PERSON
and
PROFESSION

PERSON
and

PROFESSION

Career Development in the Ministry

Charles William Stewart

Nashville ABINGDON PRESS New York

PERSON AND PROFESSION:
CAREER DEVELOPMENT IN THE MINISTRY

Library of Congress Cataloging in Publication Data

STEWART, CHARLES WILLIAM.   Person and profession.
1. Clergy—Office. I. Title.
BV660.2.S75   253'.2   74-11334

ISBN 0-687-30779-1

Scripture quotations noted NEB are from the New English
Bible, copyright © the Delegates of the Oxford University
Press and the Syndics of the Cambridge University
Press, 1961, 1970. Reprinted by permission.

MANUFACTURED BY THE PARTHENON PRESS AT
NASHVILLE, TENNESSEE, UNITED STATES OF AMERICA

to *Paul E. Johnson*

pioneer Pastor to Pastors
who taught the Professional
through the Personal

Contents

Preface

The idea for this book came to me as a result of the happy coincidence of several events: a sabbatical in which I served as a "pastor to pastors" in the Baltimore Annual Conference of The United Methodist Church, opening up some of the major problems which ministers and their families are confronting today; a conference in Arnoldshain, Germany in which a number of chaplains, seminary educators, psychiatrists, and social workers gathered to discuss new directions in pastoral counseling, but which provided deep emotional support to all present and made me aware of the need for such support systems for all professionals; and the coming together of various small pieces of research which I had done on the ministry over the past ten years. I felt the need to find and express an overall view of the career of Christian ministry today. So I set about reading, doing further research, and bringing together the material which would provide the perspective most helpful to the journeyman pastor today.

The book did not exactly write itself. However, as I got into the reading, consulting with various continuing educators, career counselors, and researchers on the ministry, the themes began to emerge. Being in Washington, D.C., it was possible to consult with some of the most able researcher-educators in the field— Philip Wogaman, Ted Mills, John Fletcher, Tilden Edwards, Jack Harris, Loren Mead, Bart Lloyd, and Emma Lou Benignus, in particular. I was further able to meet and talk with Mark Rouch, Connally Gamble, Jack Biersdorf, Tom Brown, Jim Dittes, and Mark Heath at various stages of the writing, and their comments were invaluable. The case materials from various ministers and their families were most useful in illuminating the text—these persons will remain anonymous, but their struggles I hope will prove helpful to the reader in mastering his own.

The research which I did on *Adolescent Religion* ten years ago at the Menninger Foundation provided me with the basic theoretical framework for making a longitudinal study of the ministers' work life, i.e., their careers. And, I continue to appreciate Lois Murphy, the late Tom Klink, Paul Pruyser, and Seward Hiltner for their penetrating insights into the relationship between the person and his life of work. I want to thank Reuel Howe who enlarged my perspective on the ministry to a considerable extent during the three years in which I worked as associate at the Institute for Advanced Pastoral Studies. I want to express my appreciation to him as a pioneer in continuing education who has provided a means for many thousands of men and women to think through their ministry in creative groups of fellow professionals and laymen.

My wife and four children are always supportive when I get the "writing bug," and this time was no exception. I want to thank Virginia Hamner who typed the copy through several revisions.

Finally, I want to thank the administration of Wesley Theological Seminary—Dr. John Knight and Dr. Philip Wogaman—for freeing me for a sabbatical year in which I could do this writing.

The book is meant for ministers themselves to read and reflect upon. It is meant for their families of origin and for their primary families and friends to help them understand what the profession is all about. But it is also meant for laymen who need to sit down to define their ministry alongside the paid professional. I hope young people who are considering the ministry or are in school studying to become the next generation of ministers will read it and find here a place to dialogue with its contents. Having now put these reflections on paper, I hope it hits the mark and helps the reader to become a better professional and a better churchman throughout an entire career.

CHARLES WILLIAM STEWART
February, 1974

Ministry in Crisis

A Case of Suicide

John Braun was a forty-five-year-old Lutheran clergyman working in a large suburban church of twenty-five hundred members. Born in Germany, he had come to the United States after a successful career in advertising. He had studied for the Lutheran ministry and after a period of three years in a small village church had come as an associate to this large suburban parish. He showed outstanding abilities as a counselor and besides doing a remarkable amount of counseling had originated a radio talk show in which individuals could phone in their problems, and John could respond to them on the air. The precipitating signs of depression showed at the time a parishioner of about forty committed suicide after suffering business reverses. John attended a continuing education conference and talked about this experience. He spoke of his funeral sermon—how he had made an analogy of the rooms of a house. If one is to be of help to a family of a suicidal person, one cannot stay in the living room where things are tidy and neat, but must go into the basement where one can understand the unconscious drives of the stricken person's life. He also drew a remarkable picture. He said it was of himself. In it one could see the dark colors of despair which he suffers, but the light in the back of the picture represents the light of Christ which breaks through pain and hurt with hope and faith. John Braun committed suicide the spring of that year. He himself had reached the breaking point and was unable to go on. A good friend of his said, "He simply overloaded his personal and pastoral circuits, and they blew out."

The questions which John's act raise for all of us are these:

—Who is the pastor's pastor? Recognize that the minister is a helper and counsels with people in depression and despair, yet he may lack a pastor when he himself is in need. Who helps him when he reaches the breaking point? [1]

—Are ministers and laymen at such an impasse that the professional role has become an impossible one? How may the gap between clergy and laity be bridged, a gap so large that laymen feel themselves cut off from the minister, and ministers toil like Atlases holding up the church on their shoulders?

—Are ministers capable of restyling and retooling their ministries at the various ages and stages of their careers so that they can continue to practice the profession without running out of gas or feeling like throwing up the whole thing in disgust?

—Is the church as a system capable of change so as to allow new role definitions of ministry in coordination

---

[1] Because of the inadequacy of the English language, we are forced to use masculine pronouns in speaking of the minister. The reader should recognize that women are meant at every point except when the writer clearly distinguishes men from women.

with work in the postindustrial world we are entering? Or will we remain what Martin Marty calls managers of delicatessens in an age of supermarkets?

Incidents like John Braun's suicide do not happen everyday, but they dramatically illustrate the crisis in which the ministry, both Protestant and Catholic, finds itself. That crisis is both personal and systemic. Men and women who undertake to follow this profession find it grinding them down, sometimes when they are in seminary, sometimes when they take their first parish, sometimes in mid-life. One could analyze this as some have done, as a lack of commitment or poor emotional health on the part of the candidates. And some feel that if we were to get enough psychotherapists to work with seminarians or with men in mid-life who want to leave their wives, we could make a dent in the problem. I want to take an approach to the pastor as a person and look at the personal dimension, for it is important. However, the crisis is also systemic in the breakdown of role definition and contracts between laity and clergy and the resulting conflict in the churches. The social system itself needs to be looked at, renewed, and restructured. Beginning with the recruiting of clergy, we must look at their professionalization in seminary and the ways in which they work through personal and professional conflicts at every stage of their career. Support systems are necessary in the parish, in the counseling center, in the career development center and in the continuing education program for the minister to continue as a professional.

Several principles are assumed in the text, and I want to state them now so that the reader will be aware of the framework of the argument.

1. Ministers are vulnerable to "work stress" and "personal stress" and need pastoral care and counseling as much as laymen do.
2. Ministers and their families need to spend time together developing their own systems of care and support.
3. Ministers and laymen work together as colleagues when they recognize each other's needs and try to develop contractual arrangements which get their role expectations into some working arrangement.
4. Ministers need the resources of career guidance and continuing education at every stage of their career.
5. The profession of ministry is in need of role redefinition in order to allow for more lay participation and better utilization of clergy resources in congregational life and community outreach.

Some preliminary definitions will also help us know exactly who we mean by the "minister." We are looking at the career (work life) of the professional employed by a Christian church. As a professional, this person is trained through Bible institute, college, and/or graduate school so as to be qualified to become ordained, set apart to serve as a *diakonos* of Christ. As a servant of Jesus and his church, he or she is useful in the fulfillment of the purposes of Christ in the world.[2] By preaching, teaching, pastoring, celebrating, and overseeing, the minister leads a congregation of Christians or some aspect of its corporate life. Our entire investigation will be of ways in which the minister— man or woman, Protestant or Catholic—faces the personal and professional crises which such activities stir up.

---

[2] See Knox, John, *The Ministry in Historical Perspectives*, ed. Niebuhr, H. R. and Williams, D. D. (New York: Harper & Brothers, 1956), p. 2.

The Minister Is Vulnerable

The public has labored under an illusion that ministers are invulnerable—they care, but they do not need to be cared for. The passersby at the foot of the Cross mocked Jesus and said, "He saved others; himself he cannot save" (Matt. 27:42). In a sense, all those who look on from afar feel that the helping person is either so strong that he needs no help or that he is not of the same order as the laymen and therefore has more faith, more theological resources, and is more in tune with God so that he need not call on anyone else for help.

The actual record shows however that this is not so. In the 1950s articles were published on why ministers are breaking down. Wesley Schrader of Yale told of the number of ministers breaking down by attempting to play a messianic role in relation to their parishioners.[3] Even Norman Vincent Peale published an article dealing with his own crises in the ministry, and one gets the impression that without the resources of his wife, he, too, would have broken down and quit the ministry.[4] Contemporary studies by Mills, Schallert, Hessert, and others show that in the present period that instead of breaking down, today's troubled clergyman is dropping out. The study *Ex-Pastors*, shows that only 1 percent of the United Church of Christ pastors were dropping out in 1969. Father Schallert's study of Roman Catholic priests at the same period showed an alarming rise in demitting priests, seven percent in 1969 with a projected figure of 15 percent by 1975.

---

[3] Shrader, Wesley, "Why Ministers are Breaking Down," *Life* (August 20, 1956), pp. 95 ff.

[4] Peale, Norman Vincent, "Why I Didn't Quit the Ministry," *Saturday Evening Post* (November 17, 1962), pp. 52 ff.

Mills' earlier study of United Presbyterian ministers shows that under stress clergy leave the profession rather than endure the difficulties they face.[5]

Ministers Have Family Needs

Protestant ministers who marry and Roman Catholic priests who do not both have needs for sexual expression, for companionship, and for intimacy. Statistics of divorce and family breakup among Protestant ministers and of Roman priests marrying rather than staying celibate betray their vulnerability. The problems we shall uncover—the priest who has trouble relating to women in the parish, the Protestant minister who gets overinvolved with his female counselees, the minister's wife who feels outgrown by her husband, the children who denounce the church once they leave the parsonage for college—all point to the fact the minister is very vulnerable and that one of the points of stress is marriage and family life.

Unrecognized Needs
Cause Congregational Trouble

Congregations flounder because ministers are vulnerable to stress, and they and/or their families have needs not recognized by congregations. The troubled minister may pull himself together, but he may do it at the price of rigidity, of compulsive behavior, or of walling himself off from the parish. As a result the congregation suffers. Rather than having a warm, loving person as a pastor, people feel alienated

---

[5] Mills, Edgar, "Leaving the Pastorate: A Study in the Social Psychology of Career Change," Ph.D. Thesis, Harvard University, 1965.

from him. Similarly the needs of the congregation are often more than the minister can handle alone, and yet because of his role definition he feels that he alone is the one who ministers to everyone's needs. Care is a universal need. It is built into the functioning of a pastor and related to his shepherding of a flock. However, it is not fair to put all the caring functions into one person's hand and expect him to bear the caring role of the community. Neither is it fair to expect him to care and not receive care. What is needed is the building of a caring community within the church. We shall look at ways in which this kind of pastoring can take place.

Ministers Are Lifetime Learners

What might have happened if John Braun had not only been seen by a psychiatrist, but really been able to adjust his role image in mid-life so as to find new resources to minister as well as to be ministered to? Career guidance and continuing education resources are now available for that to happen. But, you say, didn't Braun attend pastor's conferences? Yes, he did. However, he needed not just temporary support, but new professional direction which would enable him to grow professionally beyond the compulsive need always to be helping and not accepting help. Such resources are now available. We want to look closely at these resources for personal and professional development in the course of this book.

The Ministry Can Be Redefined

Ministers need not simply get sick and drop out; they can learn to cope with the crises and conflicts which they will face at every stage of their ministry. However, even more hopeful, they also have the possibility to redefine the role with intelligent and committed laymen which will enable them to quit the "errand boy" job they have gotten into and to emerge with laymen as colleagues in a ministry—both professional and lay—which is commensurate with the challenges of the seventies and beyond. That is what this book is all about—helping ministers and laymen to do that kind of redefinition and working together to support one another in the mission of the church. Discipleship as Jesus called men and women to it is not an easy task. It is what Reinhold Niebuhr once called an "impossible possibility," by which he meant holding on to a transcendent claim, but also acting within the concrete situations which compromise that claim. You as minister or layman do not give up the transcendent claim which is laid upon you to minister; yet you must work out new ways for that claim to be realized in the communities called churches. Paradox, yes! Impossible, no! I invite you to explore the dimensions of that venture with me in the pages ahead.

The Ministry as a Career

"The call to ministry is ultimately dependent on the spirit which bloweth where it listeth yet it normally requires to be brought into connection with historical forms of the Christian community."

—Daniel Day Williams, *The Minister and the Care of Souls*

From the period of the early church, leaders were set apart to carry out the various ministries of the church. Paul wisely wrote the faction-ridden Corinthian Church that "there are varieties of gifts, but the same Spirit. There are varieties of service, but the same Lord. . . . Within our community God has appointed, in the first place apostles, in the second place prophets, thirdly teachers; then miracle-workers . . . gifts of healing . . . or the gift of ecstatic utterance" (I Cor. 12:4, 5, 28 NEB). The church at its best has understood that every person is called into ministry and that no one's work is down-graded, but is needed to fulfill the mission given to us by Jesus Christ.

New Testament scholars have traced the emerging order of the church from both the council of elders (*presbyteros*), much like the Jewish synagogue or the deacons, and bishops (*episkopoi*) of the Gentile churches established by Paul and the missionaries to the Mediterranean world.[1] When it became apparent

---

[1] For biblical studies see Minear, Paul S., *Images of the Church in the New Testament* (Philadelphia: The Westminster Press, 1960), and Küng, Hans, *The Church*, tr. Ray and Rosaleen Ockendin (London: Burns, & Oates, Ltd., 1967).

to the first century Christians that Jesus was not returning soon and the Roman persecutions of the church began, they found it necessary to organize themselves for survival's sake. The clergy-lay split was not complete, however, until the year A.D. 1000 when the Gregorian reformers terminated lay investiture and imposed clerical celibacy. The church has from the beginning seen the need for leaders, but leaders who would serve rather than gather status for themselves from the office. The corruptions of power within the church have come when its leaders have forgotten that *all* are called to be followers of Jesus Christ and that there are in fact no "first-class" Christians.

With that principle in mind, we want to look in this chapter at the set-apart minister, at what is called his profession. We want to examine the work-life of the professional, called his career. We want then to see the shape of that career and the developmental sequences of the religious leader's work life. Then we shall turn to the questions: How does one enter the ministry? How is one called to religious service? How does one learn ministry? What is the relationship between one's person and one's profession? And finally, what are the special problems in the trial and entry stage of the ministry?

The Ministry as Profession and Career

Professional has been a bad name, particularly since Sinclair Lewis wrote of that knave, *Elmer Gantry,* and more recently since the critics of the 1960s (including Gibson Winter, Stephen Rose, Martin Marty, and Jeffrey Hadden) brought to our minds the sharply divisive gap between the leadership of the church and the congregation. To many, being a "professional" means being a big-time star and doing what one does for money, status, and power. Professionalism in the theater, sports, and politics has meant just that in a society dominated by mass media. It is hard to see the ministry of Jesus Christ in that light.

However, we shall use the word "profession" to mean the set-apart calling of priest and nun, pastor, and Christian educator.[2] In this light, the ministry is a profession, perhaps the oldest profession, tracing back to the medicine man or shaman who was distinguished from other members of the tribe because of prophetic and healing powers. Let us begin with some simple definitions to put the ministry in the context of an occupation.

1. *Work* is that series of activities engaged in by men and women to ensure physical survival, i.e., to gain the basic needs of food, clothing, and shelter, or the wherewithal to satisfy these needs. In an organized society, members work together in groups to produce goods and services for themselves and other members of the society. In an industrialized society those units are increasingly large and complex, requiring increased planning and interrelatedness.

2. A *craft* is a type of work demanding particular skills. The person knowing a craft is a step above the unskilled worker on the work ladder. Examples are the craft of cabinet making or, in the modern factory, the craft of designing an auto engine. Many of the crafts have been taken over by engineers who know the technology of turn-

---

[2] Glasse, James D., *Profession: Minister* (Nashville: Abingdon Press, 1968).

ing scientific knowledge into useful products or functions needed by the society.[3]

3. A *profession* is a type of work performed in a social setting which requires particular education, entrance, and relationship to one's peers and to the public. Commitment to the education, entrance rights, one's peers, and public one serves gives the profession its unique character.

4. A *career* is the sequential work life of one who enters a profession. It is defined vertically as one moves up or down the institutional system, and horizontally as one moves from one geographical region to another.[4]

More specifically occupational psychologists have distinguished at least four characteristics of a professional. He has: (1) a high degree of generalized and systematic knowledge; (2) the primary orientation is to community interest rather than individual self-interest; (3) there is a high degree of self-control of activity through codes of ethics; (4) there is a system of rewards that is primarily a set of symbols of work achievement and are thus ends in themselves.[5]

A professional's career is seen in relation to clients. With the minister, the career line must be looked at in relation to the institutions which employ him whether church, hospital, school, or board. The pro-

---

[3] Alfred Whitehead made the following distinction between craft and profession. "A craft is an avocation based upon customary activities and modified by trial and error of individual practice." "A profession is an avocation whose activities are subject to theoretical analysis and are modified by theoretical conclusions derived from that analysis." *Adventures of Ideas* (Baltimore: Penguin Books, 1967), pp. 73-74.

[4] Pavalko, Ronald, *Sociology of Occupations and Professions* (Itasca, Ill.: Peacock, 1971), pp. 111 ff.

[5] Gustafson, James, "Sociology of Professions," *Daedulus*, no. 4 (Fall 1963), p. 672.

fessional may list himself as self-employed, however, his employing groups determine his career. To study his career, one must study the sequence of his place of employment and thus be enabled to see the direction and goals of his career.

Donald Super, a social psychologist, was one of the first to see the relationship between the development of self-concept and the development of one's career of work. He looked at the various kinds of work, particularly as represented by the professions and saw this not as a haphazard thing, but as a developmental process which parallels the maturing and aging process of persons.[6]

Career Development	Trial School	Establish	Maintenance	Decline	Retirement
	Entrance	Advance			

Career conflicts can now be seen in relation to these career stages, and the personal and institutional phases of career are seen more clearly than before. What previously may have been viewed by the individual in the midst of this crisis as uniquely his own problem may in this light turn out to be developmental or phase-specific. What Super makes us aware of is the sequence of these developmental stages and the particular kinds of career problems which the individual faces at each stage. Let us look at each in turn.

ENTRANCE AND TRIAL. The student comes to theological school motivated to study for the ministry as he has experienced it to that date. He may have a variety of motives to enter the ministry, none of which have

---

[6] Super, Donald, *Psychology of Careers* (New York: Harper & Brothers, 1957), p. 69 ff.

been soundly tested. He has a number of questions regarding the church, the faith, and the society and his role in it. He is probably in the midst of his identity crisis. Studies by Erikson and others have shown the religiously oriented person goes through the identity crisis in his twenties rather than his teens.[7] He may have had an experience with a vital church and a knowledge of an effective minister, or he may not have. Therefore, he has a diffuse idea of his professional role and some small experience in church-related activities which have given him some desire to serve the church. As he enters the training institution, he must find out where he is and how best to guide himself in his personal and professional development. Moreover, it is necessary for the student to develop his self-awareness and some consciousness of his professional self which is congruent with the church as the employing institution.

CAREER ESTABLISHMENT. Following seminary training, the individual launches on a career, usually in the mid-twenties. He or she is ordained either by a centrally established denominational group (diocese, conference, or the like) or by a congregation who calls this person to be their minister. In the appointive system, one is assured of a position, often without too much choice as to its location. In the "call system" one candidates for a position and has some choice among the entry-level churches as to where he will serve. Too, the congregation has some choice as to their minister from among the newly trained group. (This part of the system is perhaps most in need of study, both by the appointing bodies and the calling bodies, since the

---

[7] Erikson, Erik H., *Young Man Luther* (New York: W. W. Norton & Co., 1958).

lack of fit between congregation and professional most often lies at this point.) Both systems put the new ordinand either into positions where they are the pastors in charge or into positions where they are assistants under a senior minister. The kinds of conflicts faced by the young ordinand will be discussed below.

Needless to say, the young person—man or woman— entering the profession full time is in for something of a shock. Whereas previously he had only a partial knowledge of the profession, either through observation, field experience, or course work, now he is expected to work at it full time. The socialization process from layman to professional now must be completed. The normal adjustment to a new work setting is compounded by the professional relationship to a public. If one is an associate or assistant, he is further responsible to a senior pastor, as well as to a board. The new ordinand has successfully passed through this stage when he is firmly established in the profession, usually for the minister after the first three to five years.

STABILIZATION AND ADVANCEMENT. Next, the young minister recognizes a fit between himself and his work context and stabilizes in the professional role. This does not take place in his first job, but after the first three to five years when he takes his second job and has some more satisfactory experiences in the work roles. The career crises of the early ordinand will be discussed below; suffice it to say that stabilization in the profession does not take place without much creative wrestling with the issues—lay versus professional conceptions of the church, the authority issues, the structures of today's congregation, and the emphases which he feels are important for the mission of God's people in the world. The new breed of clergy will most likely not stabilize easily, but will want to see change take place in structures and relationships enabling them and others to work more freely and creatively.

Advancement within the ministry takes place by working hard and productively in the positions in which he finds himself, as it does in medicine or in law where the professional is also self-employed. However, because the minister's clients are organized, i.e., hire him and therefore have some voice in his work and in evaluating the success or failure of his efforts, the laity will determine to a large extent if, when, and how he advances. This is true more largely in the congregationally organized churches, where laymen both evaluate and call their leaders. However, in the episcopally organized churches it is also true in that the laity report to the denominational leaders at least annually, and the leader is responsive to the layman's account as to the minister's competence in his church leadership. Advancement generally means being appointed or called to a church with larger membership and larger budget, with a larger physical plant, and in the "upper registers," having paid staff to assist the pastor in the church's work. To recognize the church as a social system and the ministry as a career means that one cannot fail to take account of the fact that there are larger social units in the system and stages in the professional career. The church has its "treasure in earthen vessels" and rewards its servants through professional advancement. The rewards are expressed through increased salaries, increased status, and increasing prestige, meaning the honors coming to the advancing person who has accomplished something of community significance in his work.

A minister usually advances from age thirty to forty, moving from one position to another as he achieves some measure of success in the churches which he serves. Advancement may also be registered as a minister stays at one church which is going through a growth cycle and as he develops himself to fuller stature through administering this church. In the appointive system, the bishop and district superintendent advance ministers in an attempt to bring the right person and right congregation together. In the call system, pulpit committees extend the call to those—usually before age forty-five—who show bright promise or who have achieved in their present position. Previously, preaching has been the means by which the young minister became known; currently pastoral counseling, community action, or administrative ability may be the skills which attract laity to a young pastor.

MAINTENANCE. By the age of forty-five professionals are not only established in their career, but have begun to maintain themselves at their particular level of competence. The mid-careerist, says Super, "feels no need to break new ground, either because the ground he is already cultivating gives him an adequate living and is such as to keep him fully occupied, or because he has not succeeded in a quarter century of effort to find or break good ground and has no hope of succeeding in renewed efforts." [8] That is to say, the period of forty-five through sixty reveals either fruition or frustration. The mid-careerist must ask himself: Should I work harder to achieve new gains, or should I relax some to enjoy the place I have while working to maintain it? I have established a pattern in

[8] Super, *Psychology of Careers*, p. 148.

which I have found some measure of success and achievement in my work. I have discovered what my satisfactions are. I ask: Are they in preaching to crowds of people? Are they in working with persons in counseling? Are they in enabling others to develop their talents? Are they in community service or organization? And is there solid reality in my achievements?

There are also some dissatisfactions at this stage. We shall look at the crises of this stage later. However, the mid-careerist should have learned by this time to tolerate certain dissatisfactions which the church as the employer or the work which the ministry entails. No professional career is all roses, in particular those which deal with people. The aging process begins and shows itself in one's diminishing energy and one's need to do the things which one does well; let the others go, or delegate them to a young assistant. One is vulnerable to illness and to occupational stress as one has not been before.

DECLINE. Super places this stage for professionals from age sixty to retirement.[9] The clergy are fortunate in that they may face this more openly since they may more readily choose a lesser appointment or move to an associate position which demands only specialization such as counseling, calling, or administration, and not the full range of ministerial roles. The senior minister may need to limit his activities more closely to those which he does well and delegate wisely to associates and laymen things which he formerly loved to do, but finds he does not have strength to do. Slowing down does not mean losing respect, but using one's strength wisely and well.

RETIREMENT. Retirement means not only stopping

---

[9] *Ibid.*, p. 154.

one's life work, but changing the habits and daily routines of a lifetime. It means using avocational activity not just to fill one's time, but to provide meaning and purpose to one's existence. The self-concept previously dependent on one's work role now is dependent on other roles within the community—as consultant to a church hospital or home, for example. Professionals generally have a difficult time with retirement as we shall see. Many find it difficult having worked so hard at one's profession to do anything else which is satisfying. However, the mature man or woman has made preparation for retirement and enters this stage with some sense of release from everyday responsibility and more opportunity to travel and to engage in meaningful hobbies. Persons retiring at sixty-five have from five to twenty years before death to do with as they will, and if they adjust to this they should be fulfilled and happy.

Entering the Profession

How does one enter the ministry? Traditionally, in Christian circles, you are "called to the ministry," as Samuel was called to be a prophet, and Paul was called to be an apostle. This is to recognize the divine nature of the vocation. You will respond to what you understand to be God's will for your life, however you interpret it. Without such a calling, many churches and congregations refuse to recognize your desire to become a leader of their group. However, lest the reader become confused by such language, we shall examine the minister's calling in the light of several useful distinctions made by H. Richard Niebuhr. He states that there are four distinct calls: (1) the call to be a Christian, (2) the secret call, (3) the providential call, and (4) the ecclesiastical call.[10]

THE CALL TO BE A CHRISTIAN. Every Christian has a "calling," i.e., a vocation under God. The ministry of the laity is rightly expressed here as an expression of faith. The layman does not engage in certain activities according to his ethical stance as a Christian; on the other hand, what he does in his work is a means of witnessing to his faith. Before one answers any other call, he answers the call to be a disciple of Jesus Christ in whatever sector of the work world he find himself.

THE SECRET CALL. You may answer a call to the set-apart ministry through inwardly becoming aware that God has a particular ministry within the church he wants you to handle. This awareness is tested against the calls of other servants in the church and is nurtured through prayer and the life of the Spirit. Some persons do not have dramatic calls like the apostle Paul or the prophet Samuel, but experience a steady growth of life and commitment within the church. We shall examine some of the problems of motivation below; but here we should recognize that even the secret call is of several types, and one has problems distinguishing between one's own desires and the will of God.

THE PROVIDENTIAL CALL. You should be able to see some relationship between the needs of the church and the society which you want to meet through the ministry and your own talents and abilities. Here vocational testing and guidance should be of some help to you.[11] It is not enough for candidates for ministry

---

[10] Niebuhr, H. Richard, *The Purpose of the Church and Its Ministry* (New York: Harper & Brothers, 1956), p. 64.

[11] See Theological School Inventory and "TSI Scores in Relation to Personal Background" by James Dittes and Harry DeWire, Southern Methodist University, Dallas, Texas.

to have a secret call; that call should be tested against some inventory of the person's abilities and the needs of the church. If he or she cannot adequately meet the requirements of the church, that individual should not feel he is any less called to be a Christian, but should be able to serve as a layman perhaps in areas which a clergyman would never reach. The providential nature of the call is the coming together of needs, abilities, and circumstances in what is perceived as the providential will of God.

ECCLESIASTICAL CALL. The candidate for church vocation answers the call of a specific congregation or group. The call to service makes no connection until you are set apart by a congregation, granted a license to preach and administer the sacraments, and come under the discipline of church orders. The laity have the power to call their priests and ministers, and no matter how bureaucratic a church may become, the laymen still should have the capacity to determine their leaders. How this works out varies from denomination to denomination, but the full-time minister needs to recognize he does not leave the laity in becoming set apart, but joins them as colleagues with particular "delegated functions" and is dependent upon them to carry out his work.

Motives for ministry are many and varied. However, they can be classified as either self-affirming motives or self-denying motives. These motives come to focus in the identity struggles of the young man or woman who is considering the vocation. You want to know your self, but you feel you cannot discover who you are outside of a social group. You feel a desire to know God's will not just for yourself, but in relation to human kind, and you search for a group who can join in your struggle for convictions and values. The church

—either because of close association with it in growing up or because of some relationship with a minister, student religious group, or professor—looks like the group with which you want to be identified. Why not throw your lot in with this group?

The self-denying aspects of the vocation may be appealing to you at first. You will be involved in the ministry in direct service to individuals and to groups; you will work for a low salary—and if a priest or nun, you work for only your subsistence; you will feel your service to be directly related to God's will and purpose for mankind. Henri Nouwen emphasizes the self giving aspect of the spiritual formation of the priest as "the hard and often painful process of self emptying and creating that inner space where the Spirit can manifest itself." [12] However, lest one think of this as wearing a hair shirt or living a completely ascetic life, he should recognize the need to develop a sense of his own personhood so that he can give out of fullness and not out of emptiness.

The self-affirming motives are those which are developed out of the fulfilling of both deficit and mastery needs.[13] In order to live you require the fulfilling of the basic requirements of food, clothing, shelter, sleep, movement, and so forth, and basic interpersonal security. Once you have these deficit needs gratified— and they need be gratified daily—you also have need to master some aspect of the environment (problem solving) and to fulfill your own potential. Conflicts will arise if you submerge your mastery or self-affirm-

---

[12] Nouwen, Henri, "Education to the Ministry," *Theological Education* (Fall 1972), vol. 9, p. 52. See also *The Wounded Healer* (Garden City, N.Y.: Doubleday & Co., 1972).

[13] See Maslow, A. H., *Toward a Psychology of Being*, 2nd ed. (New York: Van Nostrand Reinhold Co., 1968), pp. 21–43.

ing motives in your desire to serve. I believe they stay in a healthy tension especially in a service vocation. If you bury your talents, or act like a hurt elder brother in your father's house while someone else gets attention, Jesus says you fail to live a "grace-filled" or graceful life.

How Does One Learn Ministry?

Because the set-apart ministry requires particular knowledge and skills, the primary avenues for learning ministry are found today through the college, university, and professional school. These schools vary in different parts of the world in terms of sequence. In Europe and England the university is the primary place to study theology and the professional school to learn the skills of ministry; while in the United States and Canada the professional school is the place both to study theology and to learn the skills; and in the third world, the sequence may be to attend Bible school before university training. We could devote an entire book to theological education; however, what we want to do is to look briefly at the *what* and the *how* of learning ministry as a career.

What do you learn in theological school? Let us listen to both a Catholic and a Protestant interpreter of the *what* of theological education. Joseph Fichter says: "The best traditions of professional training in any field seem to require a level of education that includes two essential functions: research activities and technical experience." [14] Fichter implies that the research functions are often not included in a minister's training

---

[14] Fichter, Joseph, *Religion as an Occupation* (Notre Dame, Ind.: University of Notre Dame Press, 1961), p. 106.

nor is the technical experience although both are needed to enable him to function within the church. James Gustafson says:

In a society that increasingly expects and requires competence and specialization, the ministry itself needs specialization at two general points. First it ought to have a point of view that is shaped and fashioned by a study of the Western tradition . . . Second, ministers ought to have some area of competence in their work, some field in which they maintain a depth information and discipline of study and reflection.[15]

The curricula of theological seminaries have been repeatedly revised in order to take account of the need both for the core knowledge of the Christian tradition needed by the minister and the correlative connections that knowledge must make with the culture. The career of ministry will require some means of attaining *professionalization*, which means "integrating knowledge with skills in some workable role both needed by the society and able to be performed by individuals." One passes from being a student to being a member of that profession while in school, or he faces intense role conflicts upon leaving academia.[16]

How does one learn ministry? There is not one way that one learns a professional role, but many. You learn by personal study of the Bible, of church history, of theology, and reflection upon that study in the light

---

[15] Gustafson, James, "Theological Education as Professional Education," *Theological Education*, vol. 5 (Spring 1969), p. 254.

[16] I would argue with Daniel Williams who describes the use of role as theatrical. "Role" as used here refers to the social function performed in a group, not a false taking of a part upon a stage. See *The Minister and the Care of Souls* (New York: Harper & Brothers, 1961).

of your own life and experience. You learn from activities within the society—all the cultural and cross-cultural currents—which are running and their challenge to the faith and the position of the church. You learn by identification with the roles of ministry as they are worked out in social contexts—not just the church, but the various community agenices like hospital, city government, social agency, and the like. You learn ministry by supervision of your professional practice within a field setting. Finally, you learn ministry by engaging in the mutual give-and-take and supportive help which can be obtained with your peer group. Such learning requires recognizing your vulnerability—your humanity—as well as your desire to serve God. The knowledge and skills can be learned within the context of a seminary field setting. However, the integration of the social role within the life of the person will be a lifetime task.

What Are the Special Problems of the Trial and Entrance Stage?

MOVING FROM A CALLING TO A POSITION AS A CHURCH WORKER. Edgar Mills states: "Young people choose the ministry with one set of ideals and occupational images, they are introduced to a radically different set in the seminaries, and when they emerge as neophyte ministers into local parishes they discover additional roles and obligations for which they were never trained."[17] Among Roman Catholics, many of the religious decide on the profession in their early years, attend minor seminary, a Catholic college, major seminary, and re-

---

[17] Jud, Mills, and Burch, *Ex-Pastors* (Philadelphia: Pilgrim Press, 1970), p. 93.

main dependent upon the institution with little real opportunity to see the ministry in total context. A young person may reflect the various expectations of his parents, his teachers, and other authorities, and develop what James Dittes calls the "little adult" role.[18] He may be attracted to the ministry as a position of leadership which promises status and prestige. He may idolize or romanticize the vocation having had little direct experience with ministers or with work in the church. The process of trial and entrance involves getting to know what the profession involves so far as work and responsibility are concerned—trying it on for size. All work beginnings involve some floundering, i.e., making goofs and mistakes and admitting them. Until the neophyte minister moves from illusion to reality, his ministry will take on no definite form with which effectively to practice his profession.

TRANSLATING THEOLOGY INTO LIFE. Until he enters seminary, the calling of the student is to be a student. He has deliberately declared a moratorium on a work life. His problem now is to translate his theological learning into life situations, and this may involve him in some commitment anxiety. Why not stay in graduate school, he says, and study for another degree? Why not get a doctorate and be that much better equipped? By postponing commitment he may feel that he is quieting his fears about performance.

Carl Rogers speaks of a "highly intellectualized college education in which bright young people acquire a powerful technical apparatus of analysis and then somewhere along the line are confronted with chal-

---

[18] Dittes, James, "Psychological Characteristics of Religious Professionals," *Research in Religious Development* (New York: Hawthorne Books, 1971), p. 433.

lenges to emotional maturity, and come apart at the seams." [19]

GROWING A FAITH IN THE ACADEMIC/ORGANIZATIONAL CRUNCH. Two types of students are often seen: (a) the conformist or traditionally oriented student. He reflects his parents' expectations of him and may have been coerced into the ministry through a strong mother's or father's desires. Again he may have brought the tradition of his church to the seminary after little questioning of its premises in undergraduate school. On the other hand, (b) the rebellious and drifting student either actively questions the authority of those who teach him or passively resists the course set before him by failing to get involved in the learning process. Both groups may find it difficult to grow their faith in the academic or organizational structure. The maturing student, however, may question the faith and be openly skeptical about the church. Yet he is committed enough to what he holds true and valuable to be open for personal and professional growth. ·Growth means finding ways to be perceptive to your own needs, to enlarge your perspective on yourself and others, to reach out toward persons from different racial and national backgrounds, to be willing to have your limits challenged, and to redefine yourself in the process. Your faith is not so rigid that it cannot meet the challenge of new facts, nor so diffuse that it is not possible to express. You formulate it anew as you come up against new social systems and articulate it so as to take into account the existential questions you confront. Finding support

---

[19] Quoted in Williams, Daniel D., "The Morphology of Commitment in Theological Education," *Theological Education*, vol. 4 (1968), p. 34.

groups and allowing both time and place for reflection is as important for you in seminary as it will be in the active ministry.

BEING A WOMAN IN THE MINISTRY. Samuel Johnson's comment [20] about women preachers has become passé in western society, but not in the attitudes some male colleagues and lay persons have about the matter. More and more women are choosing to enter the ministry just as they are going into medicine, law, and executive positions in business. With the exception of some liturgical churches—the Roman Catholic being the most prominent—the trend is that there will be more women ordained in this century until we approximate a fifty/fifty balance of the sexes. The image of ministry and priesthood will need to be changed and laymen's expectations altered for women to be fully accepted into the profession. If you as a woman have had your consciousness raised, you may find yourself blaming men for your plight and attempt to take it out on them for the difficulties you encounter in training and entering the profession. Some of the blame may be rightly placed. However, for there to be genuine colleagueship in the church, women will have to take the difficulties with the responsibilities and be as open to men as men are to them.

Women certainly have gifts beyond their natural capacity of childbearing. Despite men's tendencies to dominate them and to keep them subservient, the young women in the ministry may find possibilities to express their many gifts in the multiple roles of ministry. Roman Catholic nuns can do more than teach elementary school children; Protestant women can expand

---

[20] "A woman in the ministry is like a dog walking on his hind legs. It is not that it is such a trick, but that you are surprised to see it at all."

beyond a limited assistant's role. For administrators and laymen to learn what they can do, today's generation of women will find it necessary to teach them. Giving up the subservient role will not be easy for them and neither will facing acceptance with no sexual strings attached be easy. Their male colleagues may help them in the process if they will.

Conclusion

"Fulfill your ministry" the writer of the Letter to Timothy said to the young ordinand. To do this you should be assured of your calling, you should enter the profession through an acceptable educational and training experience, and you should continue to grow as a Christian and as a person. Your primary identification is with Jesus Christ. This means that you are neither a little messiah nor are you a cipher. You are first a full human being, second a Christian, and finally a minister. It is a high calling, worthy of the very best and all the creativity that you have.

The Pastoral Care
of Pastors

If you fear *change*, both personal and social; if you
demand Twelfth century theology and Christianity
from your ministers; if you feel that the Christian
faith is something to be locked up within the four
walls of the church building; if you feel it is just to
hire a man and his wife—who have together put in
approximately 12 to 15 years of study and training
for required degrees to work for you, to be religious for you on a full time basis for the part time
salary of one unskilled, untrained, and uneducated
individual; if you feel that it is a Christian virture—
preparing one for sainthood—to allow one's family
to be exploited physically, emotionally, spiritually,
and financially; then you are probably a typical and
average American congregation calling yourself the
body of Christ.

—Jud, Mills, and Birch, *Ex-Pastors*

The passage above reflects a dramatic change in the
ministry in the last twenty years. In the early fifties,
the ministers reported in the press were breaking down
under the heavy demands of their congregations. Wesley Schroder's popular article in *Life* reported the
impossible role demands which cause emotional breakdown; Joseph Sitler described the "maceration of the
minister" caught in the vise between his own personal
needs and the excruciating expectations and horrendous
duties imposed upon him by parishioners. The early
studies did not bear out these conclusions. In fact the

investigation by Carl Christiansen of one hundred ministers from the Chicago area showed them to be fairly typical of the educated middle-class population.[1] And the preliminary study of Albert Meiberg and Richard Young of the hospitalized minister showed him to be typical, again, of individuals of his racial and class group.[2] The mental health of the minister did come to laymen's attention, however, and the possibility of the minister breaking down was seen as a definite possibility.

The current studies reflect a new phenomenon. Ministers, rather than suffer emotional stress which could lead to breakdown and illness, are dropping out of the profession. Edgar Mills did a doctoral study of Presbyterian clergymen who had left the parish for one of four types of work: secular employment, full-time graduate study, church executive service, or another pastorate.[3] With Gerald Jud and Genevieve Burch, he conducted an intensive study of all the men who left the United Church of Christ ministry in one year (1967) by following them up with questionnaires, personal conferences, and group meetings to add depth to the data.[4] The Roman Catholic Church, alarmed at the increasing dropout rate of their priests and nuns, also conducted empirical investigations. Eugene Schal-

---

[1] Christiansen, C., "The Occurence of Mental Illness in the Ministry," *Journal of Pastoral Care*, 1963, vol. 17, 1-10; also vol. 17, p. 125-35.

[2] Meiberg, A. L. and Young, Richard K., "The Hospitalized Minister; a Preliminary Study," *Pastoral Psychology*, vol. 9, p. 37-42.

[3] Mills, Edgar, "Leaving the Pastorate, A Study in the Social Psychology of Career Change," Ph.D. Thesis, Harvard University, 1965.

[4] Jud, Mills, and Burch, *Ex-Pastors: Why Men Leave the Parish Ministry* (Philadelphia: Pilgrim Press, 1970).

lert's study showed a seven percent dropout rate in 1970 with fifteen percent predicted by 1975.[5] The research of Eugene Kennedy and Victor Heckert, conducted at the instigation of the hierarchy, pointed out the emotional distress of clergy which was causing attrition of candidates for the priesthood, as well as men refusing to stay in the profession under current conditions.[6]

Clinical data on ministers and their families has come from a new source since 1957. Churches like the United Methodist and Presbyterian, alarmed at the emotional crises of their professionals, have set up counseling arrangements for them. Recognizing that the denominational official—set apart to be a pastor to pastors—often has too much administrative business to carry out and too great administrative power over the parish minister to serve in this capacity, the church has called a pastoral specialist to serve as *pastor pastorum*. In some instances, the church has contracted with psychiatric facilities to offer specialized counseling to those within the church who have emotional difficulties and need psychotherapy. The career counseling centers, which have developed within the past ten years, provide clinical data on clergy who are considering a change of profession. The material from such centers is confidential. However, we do have indications from their directors concerning the emotional problems of clergy and some understanding of current stress patterns.

What we want to do now is to look at full-time

---

[5] Schallert, Eugene and Kelley, Jacqueline, "Some Factors Associated with Voluntary Withdrawal from the Catholic Priesthood," *Lumen Vita*, vol. 25 (1970), pp. 425-60.

[6] Kennedy, Eugene, and Heckert, Victor, *The Catholic Priesthood in the U.S., Psychological Investigations*, Washington, D. C., United States Catholic Conference, 1972.

ministers in the parish as they report emotional difficulties and look for ways of coping with them. We shall do this in a growth-oriented fashion, rather than a sickness-oriented way. We shall look at them as they personally meet the life crises they face, and as they do it more or less successfully. Even though they may not recognize it themselves, or though parishioners may try to deny it, the minister is first a person and then a minister. Illness and emotional stress are levelers, however. If they have not recognized weakness before, when they have problems too much for them to handle alone, they may confess their humanity.

The social patterns of emotional breakdown and illness are reflected in the ministry as they are in other occupational groups in the community. Psychiatrists and clinical psychologists report today that they are seeing fewer anxiety neuroses and more character disorders. The same is true of the ministry. Fewer rigid superegos are being reported (the puritan or pietist) and more unformed consciences and problems of commitment (passive-aggressive personalities and psychopathic deviates).[7] Rollo May sees this as reflecting apathy and lack of commitment among the city dwellers, particularly among the young, who do not want to buy into the competitive, organizational society of their parents, but on the other hand are drifting without adequate roots or community orientation to give their life meaning and value.[8]

We have found at the seminary level four types of students who made the connection with the profession

---

[7] Dr. Carl Christiansen reported of 100 people, 51 suffered from personality disorders and only 30 to be psychoneurotic, the rest being depressions and schizophrenias.

[8] May, *Love and Will* (New York: Dell Books, 1973), especially chapters 1, 2, and 7.

more or less completely. The autonomous, maturing student might be predicted to have the coping capacity to meet his problems with adequate commitment and resources. The conforming, tradition-oriented student we might expect to get along at first, but somewhere in his ministry to run into personal difficulty. The rebellious and drifting student is the one who is most secular in orientation and who might find himself happier in the world than in the church. It is the neurotic and socially deviant student whom we shall encounter in the counseling agencies when he develops emotional troubles which need professional help.

The Developmental Crises of Ministers

The way we want to look at the minister who needs counseling help is through the developmental crises which he faces and the kinds of coping capacities which he attempts to muster to face these crises. Later we shall look at the problem within the social context of the church to paint in the background—both in terms of dark hues of stress and the lighter colors of support and help which are there. We shall look specifically at the kinds of emotional distress which ministers suffer and at some of the psychodynamic reasons for this distress. Finally we shall elaborate the positive resources for the pastoral care of pastors—both professional and community support for the religious leader.

Erik Erikson has provided us with a developmental model which allows us to look at the entire life-span of the individual. To this model I would like to add a coping dimension which will allow for individual differences and show the ways in which the individual, through his particular hereditary endowment, manages environmental stress in his own way. The infancy and childhood crises, it will be remembered, are those of trust, autonomy, initiative, and industry and must be negotiated at the particular developmental period, or the individual does not mature properly. We want to pick up the schema at adolescence and carry it through old age. Although Erikson builds these crises into particular time periods, it will be noted that they are not so neatly correlated to biological maturing from adolescence on and are more dependent on environmental cueing. The coping model depends on the two kinds of coping elaborated by Lois Murphy and her associates with the child study group of the Menninger Foundation. The first is "the capacity to utilize opportunities and resources of the environment to deal with frustrations and obstacles." It is basically *problem solving* and depends upon native intelligence, the ability to use anxiety constructively, and to fend off environmental pressure. The second is "the capacity to maintain inner integration in the face of stress." It is basically ego strength and depends upon inner resiliency, autonomy, sensitivity, self-esteem, and a positive orientation to life.[9]

The individual life-span would therefore look like this:

External world	Underachieving	Underachieving	Underachieving	Underachieving
↑	Coping	Coping	Coping	Coping
Life task	IDENTITY	INTIMACY	GENERATIVITY	INTEGRITY
↓	adapting	adapting	adapting	adapting
Internal world	maladapting (role diffusion)	maladapting (isolating, etc.)	maladapting (stagnating)	maladapting (despairing)

[9] Murphy, Lois B., *The Widening World of Childhood* (New York: Basic Books, 1963).

When the individual does not meet the developmental task, he may become fixated at that level, or he may regress to an earlier level. The person who does not master his particular life task will then either under-achieve or become maladaptive in the face of the stresses and challenges which his environment thrusts on him. Lidz calls these dominant themes and says: "Sometimes the dominant theme results from an early childhood fixation and reiterates, itself unable to develop and lead onward, remaining in the same groove like a needle on a flawed phonograph record. The basic themes are more readily detected in emotionally dis-turbed persons because they are more set, more clearly repetitive, and perhaps more familiar to the practiced ear that has heard similar themes so often before. Still repetitive ways of acting and relating occur in all lives. The meaning of an episode in life can be grasped properly only through understanding how it furthers, impedes or disrupts essential themes." [10]

IDENTITY CRISIS. Erikson places the identity crisis in mid-adolescence, but also points out that the *homo religiousus* (religious man) probably continues to experience this crisis throughout young adulthood. (See *Young Man Luther.*) Erikson defines identity as "one's ability to maintain inner sameness and confidence and . . . is matched by the sameness and continuity of one's meaning for others." [11] Identity, says Allen Wheelis, is a "coherent sense of self." [12] It depends upon the awareness that one's endeavors and one's life make

---

[10] Lidz, Theodore, *The Person: His Development Throughout the Life Cycle* (New York: Basic Books, 1968), p. 510.

[11] Erikson, Erik H., *Identity and the Life Cycle*, Psycho-logical Issues Monograph, vol. 1, no. 1., p. 89.

[12] Wheelis, *The Quest for Identity* (New York: W. W. Norton & Co., 1958), p. 19.

sense, that they are meaningful in the context in which life is lived. In terms of value, Erikson called this a fidelity crisis. "To what and to whom shall I be true?" is the question one asks. For the religious person this question is central since it involves not only his life philosophy, but his life-work. Role diffusion represents for the adolescent a chameleonlike attempt to change color depending upon the group one is with. This can serve one for a while, particularly with a youth culture made up of those who delay commitment to an occupational or social role. However, the adult society is "out there" and pushes the adolescent or young adult for some kind of commitment to a responsible life-style. Withdrawal into countercultural groups represents one way of solving this demand, as does delinquency or quasi delinquency (drug cultures, for example).

INTIMACY CRISIS. The intimacy crisis for Erikson is the challenge to form enduring interpersonal relations, in particular with the opposite sex. The individual in his late teens and twenties is confronted with "the potential capacity to develop orgastic potency in relation to a loved partner of the opposite sex." [13] This is represented as "heterosexual mutuality" and is more than simply the discharge of sex products. The person finds it possible to share his life at the deepest levels, to communicate his feelings, ideas, and values to someone who can respond to such communication. The Clinebells have developed this kind of intimacy to include, besides the sexual, intimacy of the mind, of the feelings, of the spirit, as well as mutual sharing of work, recreation, community outreach, and religious devotion. When one is able to do this with one person, he or she is also able to do it with other persons

---

[13] Erikson, *Identity and the Life Cycle*, p. 96.

of both sexes, although marriage commitment is restricted to one person.[14]

The opposite to intimacy is isolation and self-absorption. Erikson says the undeveloped or maladapted person is ready to "repudiate, to isolate and if necessary to destroy those forces whose essence seem dangerous to one's own." [15] The undeveloped, for various reasons, does not relate to other persons intimately and distances himself from them through various means. The maladaptive person has difficulty in interpersonal relations and alienates others or finds himself alienated from others through defensive maneuvers.

GENERATIVITY CRISIS. The generativity crisis centers around parenthood, "the interest in and guiding the next generation, although there are people who, from misfortune or because of special and genuine gifts in other directions, do not apply this drive to offspring but to other forms of altruistic concern and of creativity." [16] In other words the generative person is creative not only in producing and nurturing children, but in producing and nurturing ideas or products of one's imagination and crafting.

The underachiever is one who never mobilizes his or her potential and who therefore does not create or produce what is in him. The maladaptive person is one who stagnates and regresses from his creative genius into what Erikson calls pseudo intimacy and interpersonal impoverishment. This person might have parented many projects or made many artistic or scientific or simply human products, but has not.

[14] Clinebell, Howard and Clinebell, Charlotte, *The Intimate Marriage* (New York: Harper & Row, 1970), pp. 28–34.
[15] Erikson, *Identity and the Life Cycle*, pp. 95–96.
[16] *Ibid*, p. 97.

INTEGRITY CRISIS. To be integrated, according to Erikson, means "the acceptance of one's own and only life cycle and of the people who have become significant to it as something that has to be and that by necessity permitted no substitutions." [17] To be integrated means to be whole, and it is the struggle of one's entire life, although it comes clearly into focus in the later years. The opposite is despair and disgust. To despair is to express the feeling that life is short and that death is feared. Disgust is a displeasure with institutions, with individuals, and an underlying contempt of oneself.

The religious person goes through a "life long and chronic integrity crisis," struggling with life and death issues (Erikson). For that reason one may at the various other crisis periods teeter into despair and disgust and find it difficult to work within one's occupational identity.

Developmental Problems of Ministers

Now we want to put the life crises of the individual into a social context by filling in the background so as to understand the problems the minister confronts under the stress and challenge from the environment. A case study of a minister will illustrate the crisis and give some existential dimension to the struggle which each individual faces.

IDENTITY PROBLEMS. "He seems like he is more of a minister than a person." This indictment is like that made of the actor who is always on stage. What it points to is an unresolved identity crisis on the part of an individual who has short-circuited the crisis by settling for what he thinks will win adult approval.

---

[17] *Ibid*, p. 98.

There is no sureness or selfsameness in this person, but he must agree with those who surround him and strive to get their acceptance through behavior which he feels will please them. This began in childhood, but it continues through the turbulent period of adolescence, when he trades the conformity to his parent's demands for the conformity to the demands of his teachers or the adult leaders. The peer group which is sought may be a religious group or a community-oriented group (YMCA, YWCA, Demolay) which is either adult sponsored or adult sanctioned.

James Dittes calls this the "little adult" role, and his point is that it not only cushions growing youth against his peers and the necessity of coming to terms with their world, but grants him immediate access into the adult world. However, the youth who settles for this pseudoidentity does so at the expense and struggle of finding out what his real strengths and weaknesses are and just what he would really like to do with his life. We saw how Dittes described this kind of person in the seminary period, sheltered against the world and really unacquainted with himself. The underdeveloped side of this person is his peer relationship and any protracted period of working through the conflicts with his peers at the adolescent period. The maladaptive side of this person can best be described by the psychiatrists.

Margaretta Bowers, who had done psychotherapy with Episcopal clergymen and seminarians in the New York city area, paints a composite picture of the young male minister with identity problems. He was a lonely child, either an only child or one who did not play with others. He felt the need to carry the awesome authority of the divine (remnants of childhood omnipotence). He felt the need to be responsible for the eternal welfare of his people, not just in this life, but the next. He needed to be the center of attention not just of the whole family, but of the whole community (childhood narcissism).[18]

This kind of individual has problems with sexual identity which relate either to the death of the father or his emotional absence in childhood and adolescence. For a man, the identification may be with the mother and with the feminine side of life. For a woman, the identification may be with a minister-father or a revered priest. When the sexual drives intensify in adolescence, this individual has difficulty handling them. This person may seek a celibate life or a kind of neutral identity where sexuality is not admitted as a part of life.

The desire to please one's parents and other adults becomes exacerbated into perfectionistic drives. One is never satisfied with himself or others. One builds an idealistic self-image and sharpens his conscience to a fine point. One is unable to distinguish between what is allowed and what is forbidden and is troubled by an underground fear of sin. One's drive to be "good" pushes him into works-righteousness, with its recurrent theme of failure and the difficulty of accepting the limits of his humanity. This person sees the Cross as a "command to suffer," and tries to placate an angry God by atonement and sacrifice, trying to gain power through passivity and misery.

Gotthard Booth found that some young men who were attracted to the Episcopal ministry were those who suffered in childhood from feelings of inferiority, either because of socioeconomic deprivation or because of an inferior position in the family. Another group

---

[18] Bowers, *Conflicts of the Clergy* (Camden, N.J.: Thomas Nelson, 1963), pp. 5–6.

were those who were looking for and found security, both material and emotional, within the church. These persons enjoyed little parental affection as children and being in the church meant being in their father's house. The sexual identity of some was diffuse, reflecting emotional insecurity in relation to women. Homosexuality, both latent and overt, was discovered among some who either hid within the church or used it as a place for sublimated satisfaction.[19]

Daniel Blain dealt with the health hazards of the minister and recognized that some ministers show identity problems, particularly with what he calls a "straitjacket effect" and a "pedestal effect." By the first he meant what we have dealt with as perfectionism, particularly the drive to moralistic ends. By the second he meant the tendency to play God, to get what one is preaching and teaching mixed up with one's person. Both tendencies reflect the identity problem within the context of the church. Parishioners tend to expect ministers to be good, but he tries to "one up" them and not make mistakes. They also expect the preacher to know and be able to speak about God. But, in the intensive demands of the parish, he loses objectivity and tries to play God in his statements and in people's lives.[20]

CASE STUDY. Robert was a young minister of thirty-five. He had had a short career in the Air Force chaplaincy before he mustered out to take a five-hundred-member church in the midwest. He was an only child, and following his parent's divorce when

---

[19] Booth, "The Psychological Examination of Candidates for the Ministry" in Hofmann, Hans, ed., *The Ministry and Mental Health* (New York: Association Press, 1960).

[20] Blain, "Fostering the Mental Health of Ministers," *Pastoral Psychology*, vol. 9 (1958), pp. 9-18.

he was twelve, Robert had been reared by his mother in a protected environment. He had always tried to please his mother, but following the divorce he became very much concerned with making good grades and in leading in his extracurricular activities at school and at the church. He was inward looking a great deal of the time in adolescence. And although he appeared popular, having been chosen for the presidency of his youth group and of the debate team at school, he did not make many friends. He and another young man were chums, but neither dated nor spent much time with the gang at parties. At college, because his mother had to work, he attempted to excel in his academic program, majoring in English and minoring in psychology. He declared that he intended to go into the ministry in his sophomore year much to his mother's delight, and the adults who knew him at home also expressed their appreciation. During his senior year in college, he met and married a young woman who had the same interests as he did in the church. He went off to an eastern seminary with her and, with the exception of some difficulty adjusting to his field assignment, he did not appear to have a ripple of trouble making the grade as a theological student. He declared for the chaplaincy and spent some time apart from his wife in a remote assignment in the first five years of his work. He liked the formality of the service and was called Robert by his superiors as a token of their esteem of his flawless reports and faultless services. He remained remote from the men, however, and following the second tour of duty, he and his wife decided to muster out and take a growing parish in a midwestern suburb.

I first met Robert at a continuing education center where he came on the eve of beginning his new parish.

He found it very difficult to relate to the other men and women in the discussion group (all of whom were religious professionals). He tried to "one up" them with stories of his service projects, but did not impress the others. He stayed aloof from most of those in the group, calling himself Robert. Finally, he became aware of his whole history of trying to impress and please others by being the "little minister," and it stuck in his throat. He tried to speak of this, and he was overcome with emotion and left the room with tears in his eyes. When he returned, he seemed composed and somehow different. He said to the group, "Don't call me Robert anymore. Call me Bob." Not just then, but as the group continued through the week, it was apparent that Bob was through trying to be superhuman and did not feel he had to be a superminister. He was a human being and was in touch with his human feelings. He knew what he wanted, and he knew more directly *who he was*.

INTIMACY PROBLEMS. The minister who has difficulty forming intimate relationships may not have met earlier developmental crises. On the other hand, he may have developed maladaptively as a result of anxiety and hurt experienced in growing up. In both instances, he is thrust into a maelstrom of interpersonal relationships in a parish and finds himself a fish out of water. He lacks openness and is shut up or closed to others at one extreme; or he loses himself in "helping operations" and overidentifies with parishioners at the other extreme. In both instances he tries to hide the vulnerability of relating as a genuine person to another person.

James Dittes in his discussion of the "little adult" role sees some individuals choosing the ministry as a means of solving the problem of relationships. The role itself represents a guarded way to keep people at the optimum distance, at the same time giving the role-taker an advantage in terms of "greater knowledge, respectability and piety." The role is not in this instance a means of expressing the strengths of the person, which would include the capacity to form warm, outgoing relationships. It would rather be a box behind which the frightened person can hide, going through the motions of preaching, leading worship, even performing some pastoral relationships without dropping his guard, and being genuinely human in what he does. The earlier childhood crisis of trust was not met in all likelihood, or it was at least distorted to such an extent that this person is afraid of actually opening to others. Isolation in the study or busy-work in the office may be this person's defense against relating himself to people in the parish.

At the other extreme is the minister who over-identifies with parishioners, in particular with those who come to him with their problems. This tendency to play the savior results in a merger with people and a loss of identity. Booth discovered in his testing of Episcopal clergy that one could discriminate between *individualists* and *conformists*. The *individualists* identified from childhood with the dominant parent and tried as adults to live according to their upbringing and to make minimal concessions to their environment. The *conformists* identified with the submissive parent and tried as adults to live as much as they could according to the standards and demands of their environment. The conformist tendency, he says, "allows them to use the clerical setting as a stabilizing and directive force which compensates for other limitations. One may say that for some the clerical dress provides a portable sanitarium, a sanitarium in which the individual accomplishes constructive work of which he would be incapable in a world setting." [21]

These tendencies to block intimacy get the minister into difficulty with at least three groups: his family, the authorities, and his parishioners. We shall deal with the minister and marriage in chapter 5, but it should be pointed out that one of the times in which the minister escapes intimacy is the time when it should be experienced, that is engaging in intercourse with a sexual partner. Moreover, as we shall observe below, one may escape getting intimately involved with one's own children or, if unmarried, staying involved with friends or siblings.

Difficulty with authorities can be laid to ambivalent relationships with the power figures of childhood, namely mother and father. If he entered the profession as a means of pleasing his parents or of spiting one or another of them, then in all likelihood he will continue to parent those who have authority over him. Rather than form wholehearted relations with the authority which is to recognize his humanity, he will try to appease or fight them all as shadows of his parents whom he never really knew.

Finally, the parishioner will cause this person trouble. He will stand over against the parishioner rather than stand with him as a colleague and partner. Preaching may be used as a hostile club to vent angry feelings against those who cause him trouble; administration will be seen as a power game in which he can control those with whom he works. Even pastoral contacts are seen as dangerous, for, as we noted above, one must not let individuals get too close to one, or they will undermine one's preciously bought security.

---

[21] Booth, *Ministry and Mental Health*, pp. 107-8.

The ineptitude in interpersonal relations represents an underdeveloped area in the minister's personality; the defensive maneuvers he uses represent maladaptive ways of coping with the stress which social relations cause. In either instance, the social system of the parish is a constant challenge to the vulnerability of such a person and may cause him to break down.

CASE STUDY. "[Paul] is an associate pastor in his early thirties. His parents experienced constant tension in their marriage because of the father's petty criticism of the mother who could do nothing at all to please him. She accepted his fault-finding without much outward expression of her hurt feelings, although she occasionally shared them with this son who would one day be a priest. This built up their resentment of the father at the same time that it accentuated their feeling of powerlessness to deal with him. At one period in the marriage the father drank quite heavily. The marriage, however, endured even though the tension in the relationship of husband and wife has never been resolved.

"This is probably related to [Paul's] sudden and unexplained move to enter the seminary over his father's strong objections. He made the decision impulsively as if he were trying to prove to himself that he could do something worthwhile on his own and as a reaction to the strong controlling influence of the father. Unfortunately, this priest had two assignments in a relatively short time after ordination, meeting in each one a pastor whose authoritarian attitudes presented to him again the image of a controlling father. These experiences embittered him strongly and rekindled the feelings of worthlessness and powerlessness which he experienced in his own family life. He still labors under the burden of this bitterness, avoiding other priests and authorities and fully decided to keep to himself in order to avoid being dependent on others or having others dependent on him.

"This man [Paul] suffers from a severe obsessive compulsive neurosis with accompanying strong feelings of anxiety, guilt and personality inadequacy. These have reduced his efficiency and have left him depressed, fearful and quite vulnerable to stress. He not only feels unable to cope with his inner sexual drives and dependency needs in any effective manner, but his fear and distrust of others has caused him to pull away from even the possibility of close emotional contacts. He has become progressively isolated and self-preoccupied, but this avoidance technique has not really helped him. It has only increased his pain and frustration so that now he turns his anger at God for having let him down. His rejection of God, however, has also become unbearable because of the guilt which he feels. He tries to atone for his rejection of God but once again he finds that he cannot live up to his expectations and falls once more into the vicious cycle of helplessness, despair, and guilt.

". . . The constellation of difficulties has shaped his sense of worthlessness and self-doubt. At the present time he is not sure where he stands, vacillating between over-control and self-indulgent behavior. His underlying rebellion against a cold, indifferent yet controlling father figure seems to be enacted in his relations with unresponsive pastors as well as with God whom he simultaneously loves and rejects. Unless this man receives psychotherapy there is every likelihood that he will not be able to sustain himself in this unremitting situation of conflict. He will either leave the priesthood or he will remain and become more isolated, lonely and despairing and his work and relationships will suffer accordingly." [22]

GENERATIVITY PROBLEMS. We shall look more in detail at the problems of career in chapter 4, but we want here to note the individual dynamics of the crisis. We have seen that some men and women go into the ministry to short circuit the identity crisis, evade the intimacy crisis, or by merger or some other tactic, defend against it. In similar fashion, individuals can fail to meet the challenge to create, and underachieve in the ministry. As a matter of fact, the small church no longer provides a sinecure; but it can still provide a protective back eddy in which the clergyman can live out his days. The call to greatness inherent in disciple-ship is muffled—even blunted. Erikson calls this *stagnation*, expressed in the unwillingness to parent another generation. Such impotence has its emotional reasons, in particular the inability to try and fail, to put oneself on the line.

At the other extreme, often seen in the counseling center, is the burned-out parson who may be mentally depressed or physically exhausted. The demands that the parish puts on him make it difficult to continue in a situation where he must produce. In many instances he is a passive-dependent person who finds it impossible to be filled up emotionally. He has attempted to work out his salvation in the ministry, but because of his own dependency needs regresses to a stage where others feed him and give him their complete attention and support. When others put him in a situation where he is looked upon as "father of the flock" and are

---

[22] Kennedy and Heckert, *The Catholic Priest in the U.S.*, Washington, D. C., United States Catholic Conferences, 1972, pp. 72-73.

dependent upon him, he feels continually drained and emptied out. The cycle of never-ending work, or at least work that is not structured and limited, gets to this person and eventually leads to exhaustion and breakdown.

The inability to think creatively, to work in the many-faceted roles of the ministry, to be a parent to his own children, and in particular to be a spiritual parent to a congregation shows up in the parish. One has no place to hide, at least not for very long. One's sermons come up dull, interpersonal relations lack luster, projects die aborning. The ministry calls out the potential in a person who is open and resourceful; it shows up the dullard and depressed just as surely.

CASE STUDY. [Peter] . . . "is a man in his early forties who has begun to deal with the elements of his own growth but who has not really been able to integrate his new experience as yet. He is a socially and mentally intelligent man who, in general, is satisfied with his priesthood and his current work, if not with the structures of the Church as they are now. He has what might be described as a type of split personality. On the other hand, he is liberal in his ideas in a moderate kind of way; he can face and understand what is occuring in the Church and even look at his life and judge that much of his home and seminary education was quite repressive and that this had a sharp influence on his own lack of full development. He knows that something should be done to counteract these possible negative influences in the lives of others. At the same time, however, he is not free from a deeply ingrained puritanical and authoritarian emotional pattern of life which still influences him.

"At the present time the principal area of conflict in his life centers around his professional relations with others, especially women. Given the liberalization of ideas within the Church, he gradually has become more and more deeply involved with a variety of women on various levels of his priestly work. He is doing good work in many of these contacts. He has not yet, however, worked out viable ways of handling the affectional and sexual urges that arise in the context of this work. This experience of his own sexuality is something new for him. Because of his repressed background, he is awkward in dealing with it. He handles the guilt that arises from his contacts with women in a variety of ways: confession, discussing his problems with his friends, but also by punishing himself in various ways—for example, he forces himself to recite the breviary even though he considers this a truly meaningless task.

"[Peter] . . . also feels uneasy about the amount of time that he gives to interpersonal contacts. He believes in the Church and is a man of prayer, even though in the latter area he is having a difficult time working out his feelings about its formal structure. . . . His problem comes from the developmental challenge of trying to learn, at the beginning of middle age, how to relate to women in a mature manner." [23]

INTEGRITY PROBLEMS. The integrity crisis, like the identity crisis, faces the minister at various stages of life. He speaks about integrity and represents integrity in everything he does. Wholeness, getting it together, finding the interface between one's words and one's acts is what he is about. As a young man, he may have trouble with integrity, for he is expected by parishioners to be wise before he is experienced. As an older man he is expected to speak out of his wisdom,

---

[23] Kennedy and Heckert, *The Catholic Priest*, pp. 127-28.

but now experience may have eroded his faith and vision of life. At every stage he faces unbelief and the possibility of hypocrisy when people look to him as a believing person, one who practices what he preaches.

Erikson says the problems of integrity center around despair and disgust. The bitter and pessimistic minister is one who has been ambivalent about God and human life, about the mission of the church, and about his own purpose in it all. He has probably been perfectionistic, both as a young pastor and as an older one, and when he meets imperfection in others and in himself, this draws out his aggressive and hostile feelings. He would like passively to float through life, but finds that he cannot. So he swings between moods of harsh striving and moods of black despair. It is his perfectionism which leads to problems of faith. When he fails or others fail him, he projects the whole thing on God and experiences an alienation from the center of things . There is a worm in every apple, there are rotten ones in every barrel. He judges every experience in terms of disintegration and destruction and fails to see the constructive and life-renewing forces about him.

The fear of death and the unwillingness to accept death as a part of life are central to these problems. Inherent in the problem are the earlier unresolved problems of identity, generativity, and intimacy. Erikson finds it resolved in the individual's relationship to God. "Finally," he says, "the glass shows the pure self itself, the unborn core of creation, the . . . center where God is pure nothing. This pure self is the self no longer sick with a conflict between right and wrong, and not dependent on providers and not dependent on guides to reason and reality." [24] The religious person, more

---

[24] Erikson, *Young Man Luther,* p. 264.

than others, faces problems in this area because of the nature of his vocation. However, he has possibilities of working through his conflicts because he can face them openly if he will.

CASE STUDY. Matthew is a fifty-five-year-old Protestant minister who has served the same church for the last eighteen years. He has an activist wife and two grown sons and a daughter twelve. He came to counseling on referral from a denominational official. His parents died within the last ten years, and he recalls his mother as warm and friendly, active in church; his father, a businessman, was reserved and quiet. He was introverted as a boy and went into the ministry on the encouragement of an attractive preacher whom he idolized and wanted to emulate. He was also attracted to a young woman whom he idolized, but did not follow through to marriage when she left for an eastern college. He married a hometown girl upon whom he depends.

Matthew has had two affairs during his ministry. The first, when he was a young minister, was with a woman with whom he engaged in heavy petting and to whom he wrote passionate letters; the last was with his secretary who developed an attachment to him. He did not let this last relationship get out of hand however, but was untrue to his wife in his imagination. Both of these affairs have interfered with his religious life, making him feel hypocritical in the pulpit. Although the last affair has terminated, he still thinks of what might have been and even ruminates about the woman he might have married. Now he stays up late to read or watch television, neglects his wife, and stays to work at the church.

His relations at the church are also in turmoil, for there is a vocal minority who want him to move. His young associate listens to this group and makes Matt jealous and suspicious of what might be going on behind his back. He finds that he cannot preach as well as he used to, that the words seem empty in his mouth. He appears to lack faith, or at least what he says has so much wooden quality he wonders if his people get anything from it. Church attendance has fallen off for the last two years, and he does not seem to be able to come up with new ideas which might capture his board. Moreover, he is aware that the community he serves is not growing, and for all intents and purposes he may have reached the fullest growth possible in his church. For this reason he wonders if his critics may not be right in their criticism, and that he should move for the church's good.

Finally, he is aware that his two grown sons are engaged in practices which he does not condone. One is suing for a divorce from his wife of five years, and he is involved in an affair with another woman. The second boy is living with a woman at the college he is attending and has talked this over with his mother to the latter's consternation. Matt wonders if somehow the boys have picked up from him this tendency to wander from the fold and questions his own integrity at this point.

He is willing to work in counseling on his problems, however, and knows that coincidental with the counseling may come changes in his point of view, his relationship to his wife and family, and even with his church. He knows a change of job is not out of the picture, although right now he wonders who will have him. The counselor feels he is a good candidate for supportive counseling, that he does not seem to have prospects of radical change, but can become more whole in his person and in his ministry through pastoral care.

Pastoral Counseling
and Psychotherapy of Pastors

The conclusion of an extensive study of the Catholic priesthood in the United States was profound in one way, but simple in another. *"The priests of the U.S. are ordinary men.* Many of their conflicts and challenges arise precisely because they are ordinary men who have to live as though they were not ordinary at all."[25] Because priests and ministers are as human as anyone, they are subject to illness and emotional breakdown. They are vulnerable to stress, although parishioners may try to convince them they are above the battle, and they may fall victim to the illusion that they are supermen.

Some ministers have more gifts than others in the profession; others who are gifted intellectually and have all the craft to become good professionals have emotional flaws. Molly Harrower's earlier study pointed out that the intellectual powers of the individual may make him more defensive and unwilling to admit his emotional difficulties.[26] Emotional health is important for successfully filling the role of minister today. The minister who has a growing understanding of who he is as a person, who is able to form warm, outgoing relations with others, who is spontaneous, but has adequate controls over his emotional life, who can be creative and yet carry on routine work, and who functions with an integrated faith and life philosophy will enjoy the role of ministry. But he should not be discouraged if he has problems, and he should be the

---

[25] Kennedy and Heckert, *The Catholic Priest*, p. 3.

[26] Harrower, "Mental Health Potential and Success in the Ministry," *Journal of Religion and Health*, vol. 4 (October 1964), pp. 30-58.

first to admit them and try to work them out. How can he do this?

SELF-HELP. From the beginning of the Christian movement, priests and pastors have engaged in periodic self-examination. The daily prayer and devotional period has served this purpose, giving the person an opportunity to examine himself in the light of his original commitment and his espoused beliefs and values. The journal or diary of prayer has been a means of expressing inward feeling and of opening up the area of unconscious motives long before Freud. Augustine and John Wesley are two examples of religious leaders who found this means, not only of getting in touch with their feelings, but of formulating their thinking about crucial theological questions. The journal is still a means by which a religious leader can keep in touch with where he is emotionally and put these thoughts on paper. Setting a day apart, in which one is free from the telephone or the continuing demands of the parish or one's pastoral responsibilities, is also an old method which can be used. Rather than a church, the modern pastor may seek out a motel room or an isolated mountain or beach cabin where he can think, pray, and get himself together.

The periodic retreat with others in the same profession is another of the tested means by which a religious leader can withdraw from the stress of work and spend time reflecting upon his own feelings, the stress and conflict of his situation, and get some perspective, even some direction as to his vocation. A retreat director can be used at times; in some instances, contemporary priests, nuns, and ministers are putting a retreat together themselves. The newer methods of sensitivity and encounter psychology are employed by some to make the day or weekend an opening and trust-building experience.

My experience with the latter has made me feel that the important part of the retreat is to blend the tradition of the group through Bible study, talk about theological presuppositions, and expressive prayer and worship with the inward journey that individuals take. The human fellowship of a group is most important and is missing from many clergy's lives. To feel that others are experiencing similar doubts, anxieties over self-image, impotence in one's work, and anger over the harrassment of laymen is enough to bring one into contact with them as friends. The support of such a weekend retreat may well send the minister back to his job refreshed and revitalized.

It should be said, however, that such an experience is not enough for some religious workers. It may open them up sufficiently to make them aware of all the emotional hurt and rubbish they have allowed to be thrown on them for years. Self-help won't work with these persons. They need the therapeutic help of a counselor.

PASTORAL COUNSELING. The religious worker may well take advantage of the network of pastoral counseling centers which have grown up since the late fifties.[27] The trained pastoral counselor who works under church auspices will not only be able to deal with the emotional crisis which the minister is going through, but provide a means of working through the theological dimensions

---

[27] Hathorne, Berkley, *A Critical Analysis of Protestant Counseling Centers*, Washington, D.C., Board of Christian Social Concern, Methodist Church, 1964. See also listing of Pastoral Counseling Centers which may be obtained from national office of American Association of Pastoral Counselors, 31 West 10th St., New York, New York 10011.

of the problem. Spiritual directors in the Roman Catholic Church have served the priest and nun in this way for centuries. The pastoral counselor may be the contemporary spiritual director for religious leaders with problems.

In other words, what the minister or spouse or child may be working through is not just guilt feelings, but problems of being out of relationship with God. The minister is not just concerned with the current difficulty with a parishioner, but what this says about his original commitment to the parish. He is not simply confused about the roles of ministry; but he wonders when to be prophetic in condemning what he feels are social abuses and when to be pastoral in binding the wounds of persons who suffer from these abuses.

The pastoral counselor in each instance works supportively, insightfully, even confrontively, but always within the framework of the Christian faith and the resources of the Christian congregation. This marks him off as a pastoral counselor, distinguishing him from his social work or psychological colleague. He uses the resources of the behavioral sciences just as surely as the other helping professions; however, he adds the resources of belief and values which in many instances are central to the problems which the religions worker has. There are problems however, which are beyond the capabilities of the pastoral counselor, and it would be foolish not to admit this. Such problems, like those of John Braun and the priest, Paul, need the psychotherapist.

The psychotherapist or psychoanalyst is a mental health specialist and should be consulted for emotional crises which cause personality breakdown and illness. Which ones should be consulted? A referral should be sought from a physician or pastoral counselor who has good contacts with psychotherapists in the area. Margaretta Bowers set up criteria for psychotherapists working successfully with religious problems: (1) He himself has undergone analysis of his own religious attitudes; (2) He has had thorough training in the technique of the psychotherapy of religious conflicts; (3) He has had orientation in the theology of his patient; (4) He must regard the patients religious conflict as a core problem and respect the patient as a religious person.[28]

I would argue that the psychotherapist need not belong to the same faith group as the minister; in other words, he may be a Jew and the minister a Protestant; he may be a Protestant and the worker a Catholic priest. But I would agree with Dr. Bowers that the psychotherapist should not attempt to analyze the clergyman out of his religious faith or he does an injustice to him as a person. Allen Wheelis rightly points out that psychoanalysis is a technique of investigation and not a way of life. The analyst can uncover patterns of values and identity which are hidden. But, because it is analysis, it cannot provide a philosophy or scale of values. The patient gets into trouble when he tries to make psychotherapy a dogma or way of life.[29] This is provided by a flexible faith and scale of values.

It should be pointed out that simply because the minister has completed psychotherapy or psychoanalysis is no reason he may not have to return to the therapist at some other time. The crises of marriage, changing jobs, or losing a life mate may precipitate another period of emotional turmoil and necessitate

---

[28] Bowers, "Psychotherapy of Religious Personnel, Some Observations and Recommendations," *Journal of Pastoral Care*, vol. 17, pp. 11-16.

[29] Wheelis, *The Quest for Identity*, p. 173.

returning to the therapist. It is not a weakness to admit the need for help. It is rather a sign of strength to admit one's vulnerability and membership in the human race.

In response to the early articles in the secular press highlighting the emotional troubles of the clergy, an editorial writer in *The Christian Century* said something which I believe still has tremendous relevance.

> The ministry has never been, will not and should not be a bed of roses. The more dedicated, intelligent and sensitive a minister is, the more he will be wearied by the tedium of the daily rounds, frustrated by his inability to get things done, harrassed by the petulant, grumbling, meddlesome members of which every parish has its share. Every day he will die a little under the weight of his cross. He will be many times tempted to flee such ordeals. But he remains on the job because he knows that the parish—not the bishopric, the professorship, the executive office or any other laudable ministerial post—is the arena where Christ's battle for the world must be fought.[30]

---

[30] "Ministers Are Not Quitters," *The Christian Century*, (December 5, 1962, editorial), p. 1471.

Career Conflicts
in Ministry

Everywhere Christian leaders, men and women alike, have become increasingly aware of the need for more specific training and formation. The need is realistic, and the desire for more professionalism in the ministry is understandable. But the danger is that instead of becoming free to let the spirit grow, the future minister may engage himself in the complications of his own assumed competence and use his specialism as an excuse to avoid the much more difficult task of being compassionate.

—Henri Nouwen, *The Wounded Healer*

Harry Levinson has called the ministry "the most beleaguered of all professions." All professionals go through crises in their careers. What makes the clergyman particularly vulnerable is that he does not seek success or that he has certain standards for success in his work which run counter to the culture. Nevertheless, he is held up to standards imposed on him by his superiors or laymen which judge him, no matter how much he opposes them. Moreover, as we have seen, he has personal needs just as other persons do; he has family needs as we shall see in more detail below, and he has creativity needs which cry for expression. It is not so much the fact that his needs are so insistent, but that he feels caught in the squeeze between his needs and those of the institution. What we want to do in this chapter is look at the crises which a minister encounters in his career, to sketch in broad outline the way they can be seen from both an individual and an institutional perspective, to look at a particular clergyman as he experiences a crisis in career, and finally to describe a career development center and the use of periodic career review as resources for today's minister.

Let's begin again with some definitions.

A *career conflict* is a clash between work expectations and work experience resulting in slowing, stopping, or leaving current work activity. The crisis nature of the conflict is its fever state, its once-for-all feeling, which pushes the professional to make a decision to alleviate the clash. A crisis is a stress-point in one's lifeline of work which demands decisive action in the immediate future.

Systems stress refers to the institutional expectations, demands, and structures which impose themselves upon the individual in his work setting. Recruiting, placement, support—both financial and personal—all are a part of the institutional setting and may cause stress in the life of the professional.

Management of stress or *coping* refers to how the individual in crisis manages the stressful situation, either through problem-solving, accepting, or leaving the situation. Career decision involves four distinct factors, say March and Simon: (1) the visibility of alternatives, (2) the propensity to search for alternatives, (3) the individual's level of satisfaction with the existing situation, and (4) the availability of acceptable alternatives to leaving the present situation.[1] Once an individual makes a decision or changes his situation, the crisis is over.

---

[1] March and Simon in Jud, Mills, and Burch, *Ex-Pastors*, p. 109.

When we place the individual life-span in conjunction to his career-development span, we can immediately see how the conflicts in career can be traced to the interface between the two.

Individual Development	Late Adolescence Identity	Young Adult Intimacy	Adult Generativity	Late Maturity Integrity	Death
Career Development	Trial/entrance	Establishment	Maintenance	Decline	Retirement
	Theological School	Advance			

In other words, your personal development requires the meeting of certain needs and the finding of certain interpersonal security. However, to work within a social system, you must accommodate your personal needs or at least recognize that they come into conflict with the needs of an institution. Let us look at the developmental conflicts and then the systems conflicts as they are expressed in the life of a minister. Then, perhaps, we can understand what support systems are necessary and how they may be developed within the life of the church.

Developmental Conflicts

First, the professional may turn a career developmental task into a crisis by not managing it well. This can happen at every stage along the career line. With the minister, we can sketch this in fairly easily.

ENTRANCE. "The ministry is not what I expected it to be." As Mark Rouch concluded at the end of his study of young Methodist clergy three to five years out of seminary, this is the most pronounced and most determinative crisis in the minister's career.[2] What creates the crisis? We prophesied it in dealing with the seminarian. Partly it is the adjustments required in beginning full-time work after years in school. Partly it is the discontinuity between the job and the education for it. The minister leaves seminary with a "head full of theology," Reuel Howe says, so much theology that it will take him a lifetime to digest it. Overstated perhaps, but the young ordinand probably feels his preparation does not fit him for the job. He is not able to correlate the needs he faces in the parish with his theology and ethics and history which he brought with him from graduate school. He has been supported by teachers and an institution while training—now he is alone and apart and without anyone with whom to talk about his everyday problems. He could go to his superiors, but that might brand him a sycophant or worse, dependent on their authority. He has need of certain skills in listening, in organization, in community action, and in group leadership which he may have received, or he may not have. At any rate the crisis is one of confidence, and if he has needs they are immediate and cannot be long postponed at this stage.

ADVANCEMENT AND STABILIZATION. This may be characterized as the "make it or break it" stage. The questions faced are: Do I have to get on the ecclesiastical ladder? Must I play the numbers game? (Attendance and budget?) How am I doing in relation to John or Joe or Mary? Am I being passed by? (This is said in relation to the hierarchy and in relation to the laymen.) I don't buy the system as it is—should I stay

---

[2] Rouch, Mark, *A Risk for the Sake of Health,* A Preliminary Report of the Young Pastors Pilot Project, undated, Nashville, Tenn. 37202. Dept. of Ministry, Division of Higher Education, United Methodist Church.

with it, leave it, or try to reorganize it? The conflicts are as many and as complex at this stage as at the entry stage, but by stabilization they may be met with more capacity for management or anxiety tolerance.

MAINTENANCE. This may be characterized as the "don't rock the boat" stage. The conflicts are framed as: Should I keep in drive, or should I go into overdrive so as to achieve the goals I originally set for myself? Should I settle for second best, or is there really something special for me to do I have not attained? Look at those young bucks go—should I join them or stay above the fray? Why am I so tired, anymore? Should I give some things up, or should I try to do what I am doing, only not so well as before? Should I get into an allied field or a different type of church job which will be more rewarding than what I am doing now? The crisis point, when it does not seem worthwhile to stay in the profession, may be reached.

DECLINE may be characterized as the "Preaching anyone?" stage. Is the church really what it used to be—or is it my attitude which has changed? Why aren't people as interested in the church as they were when I was younger? My friends are all retiring, dying, or moving to Florida. Where can I find allied spirits? How can I keep on top of my job when I don't feel the old spark anymore? Why can't I preach and call and let the rest of the church take care of itself? Usually, at this stage it appears that the point of no return has been passed, and it is not possible to leave the ministry.

RETIREMENT may be characterized as the "Is this all there is?" stage. How can I be treated as a person when I don't do anything worthwhile anymore? Where have all the flowers gone? Is there a church who could use a church caller or a part-time evangelist? Where can I go where people will respect me for what I am? How can I be less of a burden on my immediate community? Is there a place where I can experience genuine community? The retirement syndrome is not unique among ministers, but is experienced by many who have worked all their lives.

A second way of looking at developmental conflict is to look at the ways in which the professional may be out of phase with the developmental task. You may think of the forty-year-olds whom you met in seminary. They had had a previous career in the armed services or in business or industry and were entering graduate school in order to prepare for a second career. The trial and entry stages may be telescoped into a short time so that the advancement stage may be started. Being with young adults may be exciting for mid-careerists, but it also causes conflicts within the individual going through the stage late. He is impatient with identity questions, with the floundering, and even with questions about belief when he feels so sure of what he is doing and wants to get started with his work again.

A third way of looking at management of career crises is at the juncture between phases. The careerist tends to think of himself as in the previous stage long after he has passed into the next phase. His self-image is slow in maturing because he does not like to think of himself as aging and as having to face new challenges in his career. On the other hand, he may have to make a career choice; change jobs, change locations of his job, or even face whether he wants to stay in the professional ministry at the juncture between phases. The crisis is then on him, and he must make a decision which will make a difference in how he manages the next phase of his career.

A fourth aspect happens when the minister's skills

and knowledge are inadequate or are no longer usable in a new position. A pastor who has served rural churches all his life is transferred into the city or the suburbs and finds his skills and knowledge no longer completely helpful to him in his professional life. Or a missionary returns from working in an African nation and cannot go back, but must take a parish. He not only experiences cultural shock in his native land, but must be retrained if he is to be of any use in a current parish.

A final aspect concerns career-line breakdown. The individual may make haphazard choices and find that his career is neither advanced nor does it maintain itself, but deteriorates. The minister may decide to leave the ministry for another vocation only to become dissatisfied and try to get back into a church position. He then finds his path blocked or at best he finds his way into a position which neither challenges him nor rewards him for his efforts. The minister leaves the paid profession to enter a "tent-making" ministry and again through frustration or lack of congregational response is not able to make his professional efforts add up to anything. Career-line breakdown may also result from sexual, racial, or class prejudice. In such instances an able woman may find her career blocked beyond a certain level of church; an able man may find he cannot serve an integrated church; or a non-seminary-trained lay person may find he is not able to live above the poverty level or break into a church of more than two hundred members.

System Stress and Professional Conflict

Sociologists have pointed out in recent years that stress is not only the result of individual career problems, but may relate to the social system itself. This is to say that the minister feels a strain between the organizational perspective of the church and his own individual career development. Let us look at the results of several of these studies before sketching out some observations of our own.

Samuel Blizzard in 1958 described the minister's dilemma as being caught between the external pressures of the church to do administrative and organizational work and his own desires to preach and to do pastoral work. Joseph Fichter found that priests, too, become caught between three norms: the bureaucratic norm which tells him to maintain the institution of the church; the norms of his peers which tell him to become a good professional; and the norms of the laymen which draw him toward building a congregation and a popular following. Jeffrey Hadden described the conflict as one between ministers and laymen regarding the role of the church. The conservative layman would rather have the minister comfort individuals and stay off the battlements of civil rights and social action movements whereas the new breed of clergy would rather work in the community to change social structures even at the expense of losing popularity with the laymen. Edgar Mills and his associates locate systems stress at several places. They suggest that the church as an occupational system does not meet the needs of its professionals adequately. The reasons for ministers dropping out of the church are not just personal crises, but disillusionment and frustration with the church and a feeling of being isolated from the bureaucracy whom they preceive as more concerned about maintaining the institution than about them. Problems with recruiting, training, placement, work roles, reward, and lay support are thus social-system problems needing the attention of the hierarchy within the system.

Ronald Pavalko describes system-stress in four ways which I would like to use as pegs on which to base my observations.

AUTONOMY VERSUS RULES. The minister, particularly the young minister, feels the need to establish himself, to develop a style and a way of relating to the congregation and the community, enabling him to do his own thing in the profession. The denominational officials, however, may feel that the minister should follow the rules and procedures of the organization, that he should not step out of line, but rather keep his skirts clean so that the church will not suffer but flourish.

COMPETENCE VERSUS POSITION. The minister operates from standards of competence and therefore is concerned in developing his professional skills, not in isolation from the church, but in relation to it. The layman offers him a position which they have developed in terms of what they want and expect and for which they are willing to pay a salary. They are not as willing to have the professional change this into something different, in particular since they are his employers. If he does not fulfill the position in the way in which they understand it and have described it, they may become unhappy and decide they want a change.

TASK PERFORMANCE VERSUS HOLISM. The minister works from a holistic view of the roles of the profession (sanctioned by his theological education and pleasing to himself). The denominational official and in particular the layman are concerned with the administering of the organization and the performance of work which will ensure its life. Counseling individuals or working in the community may be a part of the holistic view, but if they do not build the organization they are not included in adequate task performance for the layman. The new breed of minister may in his prophetic role find himself in direct opposition to his board for this reason. The denominational official is concerned with how many sermons are preached, how many calls made, and how many dollars have been raised in the budget (again, the numbers game) which may turn the professional off and cause him to raise his hands to heaven.

LOYALTY TO THE ORGANIZATION VERSUS SERVICE TO THE CLIENT AND LOYALTY TO THE PEER GROUP. The denominational official may measure the minister's loyalty by whether he attends association meetings, whether he is critical of the church as an organization, or whether he is building the organization. The minister as a professional may feel his service to the individual layman is uppermost—both in counseling and in small group work. He expresses his loyalty to his colleagues in meeting with them either in bull sessions after hours, at the fringe of meetings, or in organized professional concern groups where he is able to talk about professional matters and issues which for him represent the growing edge of his ministry. This for him is where he lives and grows and where he finds his basic loyalty.[3]

The conflicts within the system come down to the questions: What is success in the ministry? Who sets criteria for success? Where does loyalty to God and Christ's kingdom come in? Howard Ham's early study of success in ministry discovered that those who succeed externally at least—in terms of rewards of good church appointments and better salaries and living conditions—conform to the expectations of the social

---

[3] Pavalko, Ronald, *Sociology of Occupations and Professions.*

system; those who fail are those who are iconoclastic and are unable to "bend the knee" to institutional demands.[4] One should ask whether or not this study is still valid, or whether or not the civil rights revolution, the storm in the churches, the new breed of clergy do not make it necessary to make a new study taking more professional criteria into account. There is a new professionalism developing in the ministry that is reflected in some of the reports of studies in *Ministry Studies* and the *Christian Ministry*. The Academy of Parish Clergy today are setting criteria themselves for professional competence, and therefore these criteria need to be set against the standards of the institution in order to understand what is happening in the system itself. We shall return to this matter again in the final chapter, "Which Way Ministry?" and spell out more clearly what appear to be some directions to be taken by clergy and laymen alike to meet systems-stress and failure.

Let us look now at A Case of Career Crisis, the better to understand the interface between person and system stress.

Bill Cook, a medium-sized, dark-haired man, age thirty-nine, from a conservative denomination, referred to the counseling center from a career counseling center, where he had undergone the career testing and guidance, was referred to pastoral counseling in relationship to his career decisions.

He gave the following reasons for counseling: (1) to take an objective look at my personality profile, (2) to work through the question of whether I can

---

[4] Ham, Howard, "Personality Correlates of Ministerial Success," *Iliff Review*, vol. 27 (Winter 1960), pp. 3-9.

have a more satisfactory ministry, (3) to consider some related field at this point, and (4) to decide what kind of educational goals I should reach for now.

The career conflict centered around his current employment situation. A suburban church, which he and the present membership had established in a school four years ago, had taken a vote on his recall, and he had discovered opposition to his ministry in the vote. (The vote was twenty for and eight against.) Moreover, among those who registered their disapproval of him were several strong members of his board, whom he feared were organizing opposition to his ministry. One woman, in particular, had "read him out" at a board meeting, and he found himself unable to stand up for himself or talk back to her or to quiet the opposition which she was arousing.

At the career center, he listed the following questions which he wanted answered: (1) Can I develop an attitude which will help me work with strong, creative people, developing their leadership? (2) Does the stress of close personal relationships indicate that an area with different demands would be more productive? (3) How may I better handle administrative detail and leadership responsibility? and (4) What educational goals do I want now to set my sights on?

In listing the functions and roles of the ministry and ranking them, Mr. Cook showed conflict between the religious exemplar role which he ranked seventh as the way he functioned, but ranked it second most important. On the other hand he ranked parish promoter as second, i.e., in which he felt he functioned, but ranked it as seventh most important. Only in the general practitioner role (jack of all trades) did he feel he both functioned best and that it was the most important. Because of his conservative theology he ranked church politician, ecumenicist, and community problem-solver as twelve, thirteen, and fourteen—at the bottom of his order both in terms of functioning and importance.

When we look at how he handles crisis situations, we notice that he tends to put off difficult decisions as long as possible; however, he says, "I do not feel that I run from the difficult situation, nor do I seek to evade responsibility from it."

He described his father as a "jack of all trades and master of none." His father was ordained in this same conservative denomination, but because he had not been educated, he was not able to secure a church during the depression. He worked always as a carpenter. As a young man, Bill was sorry for his father, for he knew he was not doing what he wanted to, but was not strong enough to overcome the obstacles in the way. His mother was the dominant person in the home, but was one given to psychosomatic illnesses and in her middle fifties developed a mental illness and had to be hospitalized.

He feels his marriage is a positive resource. He married the girl with whom he fell in love at college, at age twenty. She has been both a "background supporter" and one whom he has turned to in the midst of the present crisis. She worked at the time they were in their first parish as a secretary. During this present time, they are considering whether or not she should go back to work in order to increase their monthly income. Below, we shall see that he considers his marriage the most meaningful achievement of his life.

In listing theological resources, Bill is aware of a "call to the ministry" which is experientially felt. Currently he is able to employ his theology in meaningful ways in his preaching and to find through Bible study and prayer ways of growing in his understanding of

God. Currently he says he would like to develop "an understanding of how the scriptural expressions of salvation and the justification by faith relate to man's psychological drives and defenses, and how the Holy Spirit would be expected to operate in the context of this understanding."

His career crisis has taken the bounce out of life, he feels, but believes once he can settle this crisis, he will not only have a sense of newness in his personal life, but also in his marriage and in his ministry.

The career guidance center asked Mr. Cook to make an inventory of his meaningful abilities and activities. The most significant fact about these activities is that they happened to him in his early life. Bill was an early maturer graduating from college and marrying at twenty and then taking his first church. He found in his success in forensics and journalism in college as well as his early success in meeting and marrying his wife and obtaining a church, a feeling that he was on his way. However, he slighted his professional training, taking only a year's extra study in a Bible school, four years later taking another year of seminary training. The necessity of providing for his wife and children moved him from his first student parish where he spent eight years, to a second parish where he worked for four years, then to a third parish in an outlying suburb where he worked for two years. These positions did not advance him vertically, but were lateral moves. His final move to the present parish was on the basis of his successful work in the city; he was selected to start a new parish in a prosperous eastern suburb and was given mission support to do this. He states, however, that in terms of dollar value he is still, after twenty years, at about the same salary level. His current position has more potential, but because of the congregational struggle and because he is working with professional people who have more education than he has, he now wonders if he is not wrongly fitted for his present job and feels unable to work through the conflict which he now faces.

What comes through in looking at his meaningful activity is that it happened to him as a young man. The activities in which he is currently engaged—i.e., selecting a building site, organizing an architectural committee, being concerned with money-raising—are not his most meaningful activities. In terms of priority, he puts marrying his wife as the most meaningful activity he has engaged in thus far, followed by graduating from college at age twenty, writing an oration at fifteen. Only when we get to the fourth and fifth meaningful activities do we get to what he has done in his thirties, namely writing an article which was published and being asked to take this present church.

In summarizing his feelings, reflections and insights, he says "I am primarily impressed by the poverty of my achievement. It seems there is little that is really significant in the list. I have apparently sought a sense of identity in intellectual and verbal expression, but skill in working with words is not matched with skill in working with people. The people with whom I can relate to most easily are those who in some way are dependent on me, and who give me tangible evidence of their support." The questions which he raises at age thirty-nine are: "How can I go about more effectively translating goals into actions and accomplishments? Am I authoritarian as some have suggested? Am I crippled in relationships with others by an unrecognized perfectionism? Can I learn to weld the administrative and spiritual roles of the church into an integrated ministry? Or should I choose a direction which would relieve me of that necessity?"

Mr. Cook came to me for counseling following his career assessment. We worked with the conflict centering around his struggle with the opposition in his church. He could see the difficulty with the woman in the parish as central to his problem, and he was made aware of his passive-aggressive tendencies and his difficulty in expressing anger at those who antagonized him and caused him pain. In the middle of the counseling he obtained a call from a parish in another section of the country. This provided him the needed incentive to leave the conflict without having to work it through to his own benefit. I felt in talking with him the last time that he had gained some insight as to why he was not able to realize his potential in his current situation. However, I did not feel that he had gained sufficient ability to work through interpersonal conflict, and that more than likely he would fall into a similar kind of conflict with parishioners in another situation. He and his wife left for the new parish, and perhaps because of the lower educational level and the fact that a building project is not contemplated, they find themselves much happier and more together. His wife found work again, and they are saving for the college education of their children.

The Career Development Center

In the last decade there has arisen a new type of counseling and guidance center in relation to the professional clergyman which has made the whole matter of career assessment easier. The Northeast Career

Center at Princeton, New Jersey, was the pioneer.[5] However, these centers have spread throughout North America so that they now have an association; and their directors are fully trained to undertake this particular kind of guidance. Other references will give you detail about this kind of counseling. What I want to do is give an impression of one such center located in Washington, D.C., which may give the reader an idea of what William Cook went through and also encourage the reader to investigate further if his needs propel him.

The Middle Atlantic Career Center is directed by Bart Lloyd, an Episcopal clergyman, who himself has had multiple careers. A parish clergyman, seminary teacher, and now career counselor, he approaches multiple career not as symptomatic of instability, but of the flexibility needed to stay alive in the late twentieth century. This is to say, such career counseling does not have as its purpose the saving of clergy for the church anymore than marriage counseling has as its purpose the patching up of marriages. Bart says the purpose of such career counseling is to help the person to "shape up or ship out," i.e., to find out what he can do better to fit himself for where he is working or to help him find another place to work—another church setting or another vocation which will help him use his talents more productively. The career center provides a structure in which a person or group may do career assessment. The means used are tests— vocational interest, personality, intelligence; auto-biographical material which is developed, as in Bill Cook's case, around past achievements, "and a survey" of functional abilities in order to get at strengths and

---

[5] Brown, Thomas E., "Career Counseling as a Form of Pastoral Care," *Pastoral Psychology*, vol. 22 (March 1971), pp. 15-20.

weaknesses. Bart has diagrammed the whole process in the following manner.

Gathering Data	Processing Data	Planning, Integrating	Actualizing
Retrospective reflective	Analyzing and identifying achievements	Developing my unique profile life goals	Step by step pursuit of planned goals
Inventorying	Personal strengths	Clarifying career goals developmentally	Support networks contractual
Sharing	Functional abilities	Developing specific goals for next 1-5 yrs.	
Testing	Values		Reviewing Rethinking Revising goals as needed
	Interests		
	Skills		

He finds that rather than taking two and one-half to four days as it does in Princeton, he gets better results by spacing the process over a three- to four-week period, allowing the client more time for reflection.[6]

My overall impression in talks with Bart were that the Career Development Center is a current adaptation of vocational guidance recognizing the reality of a career, but also recognizing that individuals face a particular crisis at particular points in their career. They also need help in assessing their personalities, their strengths, their weakness, their job satisfactions, their job frustrations, and to present for a one-five-year period the direction that they want their vocational life to take. The career assessment and development center relies on tests, but in this particular one

---

[6] Lloyd, Barton, in a Career Development Conference. Used with his permission.

they find the interview in relation to the professional's reflections on his successes and failures, his strengths, interests, and values to be the most important aspect of the program. They use the tests in conjunction with the other two assessment forms and find that more rather than less time is needed to do this. Finally, the center has worked out a group assessment program in conjunction with a Continuing Education Center at Virginia Seminary. Bart is able to work with groups of ministers and build career assessment into their thinking about the direction they want their professional life to take and the work that they are returning to. This occurs in the fifth week of the program. The general impression is that this kind of inventory dredges up repressed material which persons feel they have handled in previous stages of career; makes them most acutely aware of personality difficulties, of marriage problems which need attention, and generally gives them an opportunity to turn a corner in their personal as well as their vocational lives.

PERIODIC CAREER REVIEW. Following the lead of teachers and careerists in business and the military, church leaders are now proposing periodic career review for those in the ministry. Such evaluation has been available to service chaplains for several years. Because of their status as officers, chaplains have undergone officer's effectiveness ratings (OER) every six months for their first five years of duty and after that every year. Promotion and assignments are made dependent upon their receiving good evaluations from their senior chaplains or commanding officer. The dangers of inflated ratings and persons working for ratings rather than doing a disinterested job are manifest. However, my conversations with the chaplains at career development institutes in the States and abroad convince me of the workability of such a system.

Designing such a career evaluation program is a complex process and needs the consultative help of a career counselor. The reasons for career evaluation should be evident to those who would be involved in such review from the outset. In fact, if the working minister who is to be evaluated is not a part of the planning process, it will probably be suspect to him. As Bart Lloyd says,[7] performance evaluations should be distinguished from career evaluation. A supervisor or evaluative team may proctor the way a minister performs on the job, can make clear what his strengths and weaknesses are, and help him know what he should do to strengthen his ministry. However, a career evaluation is longer and more involved and may not be undertaken except at a crisis point in one's career (see previous section). The initiative here is with the client, and the information provided is to help him make major decisions regarding the direction of his career—or even if a career change should be undertaken.

The two big questions faced by the professional concerning the evaluation of his career are: Who evaluates? and, How will the evaluation material be used? Three primary groups are involved in the minister's evaluation: his superiors, his peers, and the laity with whom he works. Whatever system is adopted, the person responsible for appointing ministers or in recommending them to churches for calls, will need to have some access to the evaluative material. This represents a certain threat, but may be a necessary or lesser evil than no evaluation at all. There may be less threat if a fellow minister or pastoral supervisor makes the pri-

[7] Lloyd, Barton, in personal communication January 18, 1974.

mary evaluation. You are able to hear such constructive criticism if you feel it will not damage your chances for advancement. Moreover, the laity with whom you work daily can make instructive feedback as to your performance. They, more than your fellow professionals, are recipients of your services and should know your work from the inside.

The primary use of the evaluation should be for enabling you as a professional to correct your weaknesses, to reinforce your strengths, and to get help or further training if you need it. However, in an episcopal system the evaluation has some use in the direction of a person's career and in determining his or her readiness to assume a certain position in the church. There should be less politics in a system where career-assessment tests and interviews are used. Surely today's ministers should welcome periodic career assessment and consider performance evaluation as necessary as their yearly medical check-up.

Marriage and the Single Life

Concentrating on your marriage doesn't mean
being preoccupied with it to the exclusion of the
pressing problems of the outside world. We need
a balance between in-turning and out-reaching. The
close couple that turns outward successfully tends
toward success within the marriage. The couple that
works best within the marriage has more energy
to devote to the urgent works of our time.

—George Leonard, "The Man and
Woman Thing"

Protestants since Martin Luther have concentrated
on the advantages of a married clergy; Roman Catholics have extolled the higher spiritual virtues of
celibacy for religious workers. Today, there are new
voices from reformed groups examining the single life
as a Christian vocation, and we are all aware of the
strong movements among Roman Catholics for a
married clergy.[1] What we want to look at in this
chapter is the minister—man or woman—as single,
married, and family member. We shall ask: What
are the life tasks he or she confronts? What are the
conflicts inherent in the clergy as a sexual being faced
with relationships with the opposite sex and rearing
a family while practicing the ministry? And finally,
what are the resources and support groups open to

[1] O'Brien, John, *Why Priests Leave* (New York: Hawthorne
Books, 1969); and Frein, George, ed., *Celibacy, the Necessary
Option* (New York: Herder and Herder, 1968).

both the single and married pastors to strengthen their vocations?

The Single Life

Both marriage and celibacy are seen as Christian vocations within the New Testament. To remain single for the kingdom of heaven's sake was not an exclusive obligation for the clergy until the twelfth century. As John O'Brien points out, "Neither the words of Christ nor those of St. Paul are directed specifically or exclusively to priests or candidates for holy orders but to Christians generally." [2] Priests and nuns have registered a majority opinion (sixty-two percent) that they should have freedom of choice to choose between marriage and celibacy.[3] However, the papal encyclical (*Priestly Celibacy,* June 1967) appears to lay to rest any possibility of immediate change in canon law. Priests and nuns to take holy orders must remain celibate.

The state of celibacy does not make the Christian life easier or more difficult than the state of marriage. There are obvious difficulties: it puts a man or woman outside the conditions of ordinary life, namely heterosexual relations and parenthood; it puts the celibate in a spiritual position where he may become subject to pride or martyrdom; and the celibate may become isolated and mechanically inhuman as a bachelor or spinster sometimes does. But there are also creative possibilities in the single life in that one is free and unattached in a vocation of service; one can enjoy an untrammeled prayer life and a single-minded commit-

---

[2] O'Brien, *Why Priests Leave,* p. 171.
[3] Fichter, Joseph, "Sociology and Clerical Celibacy" in Frein, *Celibacy, the Necessary Option,* p. 103.

ment to Jesus Christ; and one can find a mutual support group with others in a religious house to strengthen one's vocation. At Taizé, France, reformed ministers are taking a vow of celibacy and finding in their community life a discipline and a way to make a concerted outreach to the community. The commitment to celibacy is voluntary and can be relinquished.[4] This has not been true in the Roman Catholic Church without leaving the ministry, except among certain national Catholic groups. However, the married diaconate has offered a place where men who had married and had families could practice ministry without complete ordination. The sociologist, Joseph Fichter, predicts, "If and when the Catholic clergy is allowed the freedom of choice to marry, the men who elect the option will be in the younger marriageable age bracket. This means that the celibate bishops who now say they have difficulty in understanding the lower echelon priest will have greater difficulty in understanding the problems of married priests." Fichter thinks the celibate priests would get promotions and the married priests would stay at the bottom of the ecclesiastical ladder.[5]

There are men and women workers in Protestant churches who do not take the vow of celibacy, but who find the single life imposed on them by circumstance. One could wish that Protestant church bodies gave more thought to the plight of such workers and offered them more recognition and support. I once met a single woman at a continuing education center at which she was the only representative of her sex at the conference. She had a very difficult time confronting the

---

[4] Thurian, Max, *Marriage and Celibacy* (London: SCM Press, 1959).

[5] Fichter, "Sociology and Clerical Celibacy," p. 122.

chauvinism of her fellow clergy. After she had worked it through at the conference, I asked her to put her thoughts on paper. She wrote:

When trying to explore the nature of someone such as myself, men ask me if I would like the things that a man could give me in marriage, and if I don't feel the need to lean on the strength of a man. Of course I do! I long to be loved and to love. I feel no shame to admit that I have perfectly normal needs and desires, the feelings of any woman. All my adult life I have wanted children of my own, but instead I teach and minister to other people's children, and buy toys for god-children or nieces and nephews. However, my life is neither empty nor meaningless, for I am busy and I am interested in many ways, by travel, theatre, music, and just visiting friends. I know that I am neither more nor less lonely than married people, for loneliness is a human condition of all regardless of marriage status.

Many times I wish there were a man upon whom I could lean, someone to guide me and help me to make decisions about major personal matters, and I am always aware of a feeling I need to be 'protected,' to have a man take care of me. But because there is no such man I get along on my own or I lean on several other people to some degree. For instance, an older brother helps me to keep my car in running condition by instructing me what to do about that strange mass of shapes which languish under the hood, but I always feel that a man would get far more efficient service from the mechanic than I do. Although I lean on several close friends, men and women, in different ways and for different reasons, the trick is to know where I can lean without distressing anyone. A close friend, a medical doctor, can tell me that he loves me without any threat to his wife and children, but when he does say this it does wonders to rebuild my damaged ego. . . . It is this kind of experience that makes the Christian Gospel make sense to me. As the apostles were strengthened and empowered by their contact with Christ, I believe that it is God's love and acceptance transmitted to me through his people that empowers me.[6]

Thank God the women's movements are not only correcting injustices suffered by single women, but providing them a group within which they may find emotional support. The church itself will need to set its house in order for women to respond to its call to service, feeling that they will be recognized as colleagues in ministry.

Marriage and Ministry

Protestant ministers—both men and women—marry and consider their marriage to be a serious vocation, i.e., a commitment taken before God, with life-long and exclusive vows to one another.

The minister's marriage like that of any layman is a role system and will develop as it satisfies the needs of each person for love and security and the couple are able to work out their respective roles in the partnership. As Don Jackson wisely points out, "to live in reasonable harmony, the spouses negotiate with respect to their behavior and responsibilities." He calls this a *quid pro quo* agreement.[7] I have called it a role relationship based upon role expectations and behaviors negotiated and agreed upon. There is a

---

[6] Davis, Ann [pseudo], "A Single Woman Speaks up about Ministers," *Pastoral Psychology*, vol. 18 (December 1967), p. 41.

[7] Jackson, D., and Lederer, William, *Mirages of Marriage* (New York: W. W. Norton & Co., 1968), p. 17.

homeostasis or balance which develops in the relationship so long as it is working; when it is not in balance a runaway develops, which means the partners are unhappy in conflict or have repressed their feelings so that they are half alive even though the marriage continues.[8]

Virginia Satir carries the systems concept into understanding the family.

According to the concept of family homeostasis, the family acts so as to achieve a balance in relationships. Members help to maintain this balance overtly and covertly. The family's repetitious, circular, predictable communication patterns reveal this balance. . . . When the family's homeostasis is precarious, members exert much effort to maintain it.[9]

The systems concept of marriage does not abrogate personality dynamics, but understands each person attempting to satisfy his own needs for intimacy, companionship, security, and family life within an interactive patterning. When one puts a marital system into a larger church system, it becomes possible to understand the push and pull, the demands and counter demands which we shall describe below. The couple can relate with husband dominant and wife submissive or with wife dominant and husband submissive in any of the above situations. The husband may be dominant at work and submissive at home as often happens in ministerial families. Or, the couple may attempt a companionate marriage and relate as peers in any of the above situations. Finally, the couple can

[8] Stewart, Charles W., *The Minister as Marriage Counselor*, (Nashville: Abingdon Press, 1970), p. 35.

[9] Satir, Virginia, *Conjoint Family Therapy*, rev. ed. (Palo Alto, Calif.: Science & Behavior, 1967), p. 1.

form a symbiotic union with strong neurotic characteristics in any church setting. Though we shall look at the conflict areas in detail, we should understand that many mature marriages are found in parsonages and serve as beacon lights for those in the parish.[10]

The Minister's Family

We can discover the patterns of spouse involvement in the church by looking at the exhaustive study of William Douglas in *Ministers' Wives*. To his list of five relationship patterns between minister and spouse I would add one more.

1. The teamworker with her husband forms a team, dividing responsibility at some points and sharing responsibility at others. She feels "called to witness, to serve, to minister in the broadest sense." [11]

2., 3. The background supporter who works "in the wings" supporting her husband both at church and in her role as wife and mother. Douglas finds two types of such wives: "the purpose motivated," who operates from her beliefs, and the "useful-work-oriented," who operates from her desire to contribute something useful to the church.

4., 5. The detached wife feels no more involved in the life of the church than if her husband were in another profession. Again Douglas found two types: the "detached-on-principle" who is not involved in church

---

[10] The homosexual alliance between a clergy person and one of the same sex needs to be acknowledged, although I shall not deal with it in this context. Certain judicatories are facing homosexuality in an enlightened fashion, particularly in the face of the new psychiatric evaluation that this pattern is not a sickness.

[11] Douglas, *Ministers' Wives* (New York: Harper & Row, 1965), p. 33.

work because she feels this is not her job. The second type is not involved because she "rebels" against the demands of the local congregation on her time and energy.

6. The sixth type I would add is the working wife. Douglas reported at the time of his study that three percent of those wives under thirty-five were holding full-time jobs and nineteen percent part-time jobs.[12] No more recent statistics are available, but if my eastern sample holds up, there are approximately fifty percent of the parsonage wives working. I would surmise that through woman's liberation they are able now to work without congregational censure. In fact I would suppose this group to increase the "detached-on-principle." In this sixth group I would also put the husband of the clergywoman who has accepted an appointment or received a call to a church. He can be a layman, or he can be a clergyman. In both instances, the dynamics of church involvement are different.

The family patterns which are represented by these six types reflect more than the spouse's involvement in the church, but the ministerial couples' involvement with one another. The teamworkers believe that the church has hired both of them and they go to work as a team. Their marital and work roles are coordinated; they share the work of the church and they also share more actively in the work at home. I know of several instances where the wife took her turn preaching, and the laymen thought her to be better at it than her

---

[12] Douglas, *Ministers' Wives*, p. 43. Douglas based his conclusions on a national sample of 38 denominations, representing a 5% sample of the national population. He sent out 8,000 questionnaires for which he received 4800 returns. On his open-ended sample he sent out 800 questionnaires and received 600 returns. He also interviewed ministers' wives at 6 locations across the U.S.

husband. Whether there are problems in the marriage depends somewhat on how their work is going, how prepared each feels for his task, and the personal dimensions of their marriage. This is a low-church evangelical pattern, Douglas discovered.

The background-supporter wife reflects a home where the husband is dominant so far as his work is concerned. His wife may see her task as providing a good home for him and the children and works in the church only in a supportive noncompetitive fashion. The purpose-motivated wife does this more out of conviction, whereas the work-oriented wife may feel unsure of herself, but feels she can contribute useful work. The middle-of-the-road churches liturgically and theologically reflect this pattern, Douglas found.

The detached wife reflects two kinds of family pattern. The first, "on principle," is one in which the wife probably is convinced that her marriage and family life are like that of any layman. Just as she will not volunteer for more work than any other layman, she also feels that she should be treated similarly so far as her home and family are concerned. The rebellious wife may decide to wear short-shorts to the supermarket or to demonstrate for busing in a southern town out of her strong feelings that she has been put into a role box by her husband or by the church. The detached wife may find herself more at home in the "high church," whether Episcopalian or Presbyterian, where they want a queen of the manse. On the other hand her rebellion may reflect itself in the general mood of women in some urban parishes.

The working wife may be working because her consciousness has been raised, or she may be working out of necessity to get more money for older children to attend college. In any case, she has escaped some of the fishbowl atmosphere of the parsonage, but has given it up for the competitive life of the community. This will reflect itself in the marriage since there is less time for church responsibilities, for entertaining in the parsonage, and for her husband and family in general. If she feels more of a person and feels that her contribution is not overshadowed by her husband's prestige in the parish, it can serve as a growing prod for the marriage.

Family Life Cycle

Evelyn Duvall developed a family life cycle, which can be placed parallel to Erikson's individual life cycle to see the relationship between the two life processes.

Identity	Intimacy	Generativity ——→				Integrity ——→	
courtship	wedding to 1st baby	parents of preschool age	parents school age	parents teen-age	launch	empty nest	retirement to death of spouse

There is a developmental task for each stage of marriage and the family as there is for individual growth. However, in this instance, the couple or parents and children face the task together and not just the individual alone.[13]

COURTSHIP. The developmental task is for the couple to relate as partners, testing their compatibility and complementariness. To be compatible means to have similar backgrounds, activities, and interests. This brings a couple together: both are Episcopalian, middle class, alumni of the same college, tennis buffs, and mad

---

[13] Duvall, *Family Development* (Philadelphia: J. B. Lippincott Co., 1971), pp. 5–9.

about opera. To be complementary, on the other hand, is to recognize their personality differences: he is an extrovert, she an introvert; he has a quick temper, she is even-tempered; he is an artistic person, she more practical and down-to-earth in her approach. But they fit like hand-in-glove in their partnership. Establishing a working relationship that can become a marriage covenant is the task of this stage, and is more or less completed at the time of the wedding.

WEDDING TO FIRST BABY'S BIRTH. The task of the first years of marriage is to become a married couple, which means to change from the single to the married state. The couple should have established their own personal identity before attempting to establish an intimate relationship. Say the Clinebells:

> Because marriage is potentially the most totally intimate of human relationships it is both the most difficult relationship, on the one hand, and the most rewarding on the other. It is the place where most adults have the opportunity to lessen their loneliness, satisfy their heart hungers, and participate in the wonderfully creative process of self-other discovery.[14]

The role system they establish is dependent on their ability to communicate openly and to adapt and to adjust to each other's needs and the marriage's demands.

PARENTS OF PRESCHOOL CHILDREN. The task is for the couple to learn the skills and roles of mother and father demanded by the birth or adoption of a child. Their previous success in adapting and adjusting to one another and to the business of living together will serve as the basis for successful coping with this task. Time is needed for the couple's learning the husband/

---

[14] Clinebell and Clinebell, *The Intimate Marriage* (New York: Harper & Row, 1970), p. 18.

wife role before they attempt the mother/father role, which argues for putting off having children for a year or two after the wedding.

PARENTS OF SCHOOL CHILDREN. The task of the oldest child sets the task for the family. When the child starts to school, mother and father must let him go and begin to learn within the larger community. The father serves as a role model for his son, the mother for her daughter. The parent's marriage is under constant observation by the child as he learns the ways of men and women.

PARENTS OF ADOLESCENTS. The developmental challenge is to set the child free to learn the tasks of adolescence—finding his identity, relating to the opposite sex, learning about the world of work, and so forth. The couple should have been developing their own relationship as the child becomes a youth, for again, he identifies with the parent's marriage as a model for his own heterosexual unions.

LAUNCHING STAGE. Parents of young men and women who start off to college or leave home to begin work cut the ties with children without losing track of them. The floundering stage many youth go through—whether it be wandering through the country or living in a commune or becoming a part of the counterculture—must not only be accepted by parents at this stage; they must allow the young adult to learn who he is and what he really wants to do with his life.

EMPTY NEST. The couple whose children have left home and married face an acute crisis in their relationship. The woman, if her identity has been primarily as a mother and background supporter, may need to consider a second career. The husband may face his own career crisis—as we observed in the last chapter—and some major changes may need to be made. Many times the marriage itself needs to be reconstituted in order to survive.

RETIREMENT TO DEATH OF ONE SPOUSE. The couple facing retirement face it together and need to find meaningful activities in their mature years. As we observed in the last chapter, an individual has either found wisdom by this period, or he faces emotional problems—depression or despair. Erikson called the opposite of wisdom or integrity disgust, and one sees it in couples as well as individuals who have lost the freshness and vitality from their marriages. When one partner dies, the other—husband or wife—faces the necessary grief and active adjustment to single life which that necessitates. Care needs to be taken to leave the other in secure financial condition and with suitable retirement living conditions.

Conflicts of a Clergy Couple

The clergy couple, until fairly recently, has been able to keep their conflicts submerged, or at least out of public awareness. The royalty complex that ministers ought to be cardboard saints was not only a lay expectation, but a clergy hang-up. The minister found it hard to admit that he, his wife, and his family had troubles like other human beings. Many social forces have operated to bring the clergyman to an awareness of his humanity: the lay renaissance, women's liberation, the decline of victorian morality, the counseling emphasis in his training to name a few. His wife is not a Norah who lives in a "Doll's House," but is a growing person who certainly needs all the attention and room to grow that any other parishioner has.

Without being exhaustive as to the kinds of conflicts clergy couples face, one can describe several marriage situations so as to understand the particular pressures of a professional family. After having done this, we can better understand the kind of helping resources which are available to work through the conflicts and more creatively cope with the pressures.

THE OUTGROWN WIFE. William White first drew attention to this phenomenon in relation to the businessman who marries someone "on the way up" and after he makes it to the top finds that he has outgrown his wife. The professional, on the other hand, may marry his childhood sweetheart while in college, and then go on to his professional training while his wife works to put him through. More often than not, for the seminary student, his wife will not be able to attend his very interesting classes in theology and Bible and finds that she does not share an important part of his life. This can become a source of conflict after the husband has completed his training. In fact, I have known of at least a dozen couples where the marriage breaks up at this point. The wife feels inferior in the very area in which her husband has competence; the fact that she has worked to enable him to obtain his training makes it the more galling; she may resent the seminary and the time he spends in the study. The first years in the parish may be enough to bring the conflict out in the open if they have not faced it during the seminary years.

THE HARRIED MATE. The young minister in the entrance and advancement years (see chapter on "Career Development") must work long and hard to become competent in his work and to obtain some status with peers as a professional. The nine to five hours of many office workers is not the pastor's lot, nor is the long weekend which many young couples use to get connected again after the ravages of the work week.

This is obvious to an outsider, but one engaged in the ministry, for example, may unconsciously neglect his wife until she gets angry at him and blows up over "just one more meeting." Taking a day off may have been one of his promises at the beginning; but it gets swallowed up in the general business of running the parish. The telephone calls during dinner become not just an annoyance, but a wedge which is driven between husband and wife.

Another side of this problem concerns ministers who find themselves getting cool towards the spouse and retreating to the church study or using a busy schedule as an excuse to stay away. The drying up of affection between them and the neglect of their sexual life are symptomatic of the harried mate's use of business as a retreat from the marriage. The "trapped wife" names the reactive pattern for the woman who pours herself into her housework, or her family, or "good works" to assuage the hurt she feels by being neglected. Underneath she resents being trapped into a static marriage where the intimate sharing she expected is now absent, and there appears no way of regaining it.

THE ABSENT PARENT. The minister with a family may, during the advancement years or at any stage of his career, neglect the children more completely than he does the spouse. Because of the pressures of work, the minister expects the partner to be both mother and father to the children. I have heard ministers' spouses actually say that their young children ask who the stranger is who spends time at their home on Saturday mornings. Of course it's their parent, but the minister is so wrapped up in work that he spends no time with them, or he fails to make the kind of emotional investment that will make a difference in their lives. Resentment of the church can grow in children's minds which may emerge as active rebellion in adolescence. However, the more serious effect is the lack of a role model for young people growing up in the parsonage and the possibility that both boys and girls will have difficulty with marriage because they see so little of one side of it while they are growing up.

THE MID-LIFE MARRIAGE. Clergy couples have the same difficulty that other couples have at mid-life although they may not recognize it. When the children leave home for college or work, the couple may find that the intimacy they thought they shared is absent. They have passed each other like ships in the night, and the reasons for their being married in young life they no longer obtain. Another way of saying this is that they have not developed a companionship which can sustain them during the last half of their life. They can keep up appearances for the sake of the church, but this is a hollow pretense which probably does not escape the notice of their parishioners. Marriage counselors have discovered that next to the first year of marriage, the twentieth year is the most dangerous. The husband or the wife may have an affair, may decide to separate, or may get ill from the emotional pressures of the marriage. On the other hand, this can be one of the most creative times during a marriage, but not without adequate assessment by the couple and active coping with what they face.

FIDELITY AND INFIDELITY. One of the serious difficulties is the fact that the minister-husband may find other women attractive, and that the minister-wife may find other men available when her husband is not. The minister-husband who is a "womanizer" can be highly popular, but if he is to act out his sexual problems by taking a mistress or by playing around with women in the parish, he will not only cause his wife difficulty, but he will find it difficult to remain a shepherd of the whole flock. Similarly, the wife who for her own emotional reasons finds herself a lover will cause her husband difficulty and before the affair is over wreak havoc upon her marriage. Some young clergy couples are trying to work out open marriages which allow for friendships with the opposite sex. This offers freedom to move out of a static marital system where they feel vulnerable to the "grass widows" and Lotharios of the community. However they view fidelity, the parish will expect moral rectitude of minister and spouse. If there are sexual problems on the part of either of them, they should seek professional counseling rather than be open to difficulty in this area.

THE PASSED-BY SYNDROME. The minister who does not make it professionally will no doubt have problems with spouse and family. We noted the problem from the career point of view in the last chapter; however, it is necessary to see the effect here on the family. The financial squeeze is probably most evident: This minister stays at smaller churches and therefore does not rise above the minimum salary. And, as Edgar Mills' studies have shown, in 1970 this was about seven thousand dollars, which is less than a nurse or a beginning schoolteacher earns. The minister's family does not have what other families in the parish have; they must get along with second-hand cars, inferior clothing, and none of the advantages other families have. The college education of the children is a precarious thing to finance; health care is difficult to handle in a crisis. Psychologically, the pastor feels defeated; the spouse is frustrated and may take this out on the minister or the children. If the spouse works it may be in a menial job which does not give them much esteem or feeling that they as a family are getting anywhere.

The families whom I have counseled with this problem are most difficult to reach because the causative factors are so complex and often so hard to change. The marriage may be in trouble, and in particular, children may be acting out their frustrations in antisocial behavior in these families. This may be an instance of a "copeless" family; their coping abilities appear to be frozen; they appear to be locked into their troubles.

THE DIVORCED MINISTER. Depending upon his denominational polity and the nature of the congregation he serves, the divorced minister will find his personal crisis compounded by the pressures put upon him by laymen. Added to his own value system regarding the permanency of marriage are the expectations that he will somehow be above this most human problem. He has performed the layman's marriage, baptized his children, taught his young people, and is therefore expected to represent the enduring quality of the Christian home.

Seward Hiltner submitted a questionnaire to a number of divorced ministers in 1966. One who wrote back anonymously has this to say to those who think about being divorced while serving a church.

He will need to weigh carefully the answer to certain questions: Can he stand the emotional strain of divorce proceedings and the aftermath? Will the church accept him as a divorced pastor? What does his denomination and its leadership say, officially and unofficially? Would an unhappy marriage be less a burden than a divorce? What was the real cause of the failure of his marriage? Would he be better off to leave the ministry? Should he remarry? What of the children? [15]

---

[15] Anonymous, "The Effect of a Divorce on a Minister's Life," *Pastoral Psychology*, vol. 18 (December 1967), pp. 35-36.

Some ministers who have established themselves with a congregation may weather a divorce and stay with the parish. However if a minister finds it necessary to take another position, it should be done with good will and a genuine attempt at personal and professional renewal. Before divorce, a minister and his spouse should surely seek counseling help.

Counseling with Clergy in Marital Conflict

Where does a ministerial couple seek help when their marriage is in trouble? And what kind of help will they receive once they seek it? First, we should say that for a minister and spouse to seek help is not a sign of weakness, but may be a recognition that they have growing pains in their marriage, that they need someone beside themselves to talk with, or that they are in a tangled web of relationships which needs an impartial third person to help unravel. The pastor more easily recognizes this situation in parishioners than in himself. His partner may need to sound the alarm, to let him know about dissatisfactions so that notice is taken that their marriage needs some attention.

Where may the ministers and their partners go for help? The pastoral counseling centers described in the last chapter represent one such resource. The statistics reported by Dr. Leroy Graham after ten years of operation of the Washington Pastoral Counseling Center (United Methodist) reveal that seventy-five percent of the clergy who seek help have marriage and family problems. The couple may go to a social agency— Family and Children's Services is one—where social workers especially trained in marriage and family counseling are able to provide counseling. Many community health centers now are staffed with counselors who can help the couple needing counseling. Finally, one or both parties may need to seek a psychotherapist to help him with emotional distress which affects the marriage. Even were a couple to go to a pastoral counseling center, social agency, or mental health center, they could be referred for psychotherapy if one or the other appeared to need more than marriage counseling because of the neurotic aspects of the problem. Once they seek help, the clergy couple should persevere, even though church business or family pressures intrude. Their marriage is as important as any in the parish and needs as much nourishment and care as any layman's does.[16]

The Marriage Counseling Process

What can the couple expect when they once go to a marriage counselor? Depending upon the helper, they may be seen individually or conjointly. The majority of the counselors who belong to the American Association of Marriage and Family Counselors practice a "systems approach" and believe that for the marriage to be helped, both partners must be seen. I have elaborated a role relationship approach in *The Minister as Marriage Counselor*. The goals of relationship counseling are: "(1) to help the client to understand his role image—this is, his picture of his role—the role expectations of others in his social orbit, and of his role behavior in his social context, for example his family; (2) to see the conflict between his role expectations and his actual behavior in the role,

---

[16] See Oates, Wayne, *Where to Go for Help*, rev. enl. ed. (Philadelphia: The Westminster Press, 1972), for specific guide for Counseling Resources.

both from his own viewpoint and from that of the significant people in his environment; (3) to develop alternative ways of handling himself, and either to change or adjust his role image and behavior." [17]

To illustrate the process, let us look at the marriage of John and Susan, a young married couple still in graduate school. John is a Roman Catholic and is obtaining his master's degree in theology. He expressed to the counselor that he wants to become a lay theologian for a metropolitan council of churches. Susan is planning to be ordained and wants to serve as a Protestant pastor. They cannot decide whose career they should follow; i.e., who should accept the first call, and who should adjust his (her) career to the other person's. The role conflict between breadwinners is in evidence; however, this couple does not want to resolve these conflicts in a traditional way, but have come to a marriage counselor to discuss what two careers in ministry mean.

The role of the counselor is threefold: (1) he *appraises* the marital problem in its current manifestation, getting some impressions of the role relationship of the couple and what appears to be going wrong in the marital system; (2) he *intervenes* in the marriage at the appropriate time with his presence, support, and remarks, serving as limit setter, clarifier, constructive catalyst, and modifier of behavior; (3) he *enables* the couple to make the necessary changes in their relationship so that they may negotiate a new marriage contract. Finally, he terminates the counseling. Like the parent or teacher he does not foster dependence, but works to enable the couple to make it on their own.

---

[17] Stewart, *The Minister as Marriage Counselor* (Nashville: Abingdon Press, 1970), p. 36.

Let us imagine a second couple who are in a special room equipped with a one-way screen where we can see them in process of counseling. This is not an actual couple, but a composite picture of several clergy couples whom I have seen.

Appraisal Stage. Bill and Ann tell the counselor that they are in their first church, having been called last summer. It is now December. They were married the previous year during Bill's last year in seminary, and both had worked part time as youth ministers in a suburban church. They are now in a small, rural charge outside a large, metropolitan area. They say that their first year of marriage has meant not only adjusting to one another as marriage partners, but finding their work roles in the parish. To add to the difficulty, Ann had been married before and brought a young girl, age two, into the marriage. The counselor appraises the situation by hearing both parties out as to their version of the conflict. Bill says, with some forcefulness in his voice and posture, that he wants to dominate in the church and does not want Ann to interfere in parish problems. Ann is burdened with the baby, but wants to be allowed into Bill's world. She has tended to shut him out of the nursery. In the heat of the quarrel she has also refused Bill sexual relations. Their families have tried to interfere—Bill's by offering them advice as to the conduct of their church work, and Ann's by buying the baby clothes when Bill's modest salary would not allow it. The counselor gets the conflict out on the table by asking what each wants of the other and what about one's behavior frustrates the other. He observes their style of fighting, in particular the constructive and destructive quality of it. (Constructive quarreling is problem-solving in dead earnest under the heart of emotion; destructive quarreling is attacking the person of the other, in particular his weak points.) He helps Bill to be aware that his attacks on Ann's family are destructive and that Ann's withdrawal of sex is a counterattack against Bill's hurting her.

Intervention. The counselor attempts to get Bill and Ann to begin to solve their problems constructively. They are hurt, but they both desire to reconcile and so want to try another way to get through to the other and to begin to work together on their problems. They learn to establish ground rules for their discussions, to tell each other where the sensitive areas are which they do not want to bring into the discussion, where they are frustrated and want some relief from the other, and what they now want of a positive nature from the partner. The counselor teaches Bill and Ann to "fight fair" to use George Bach's term.[18] The fight cycle is rehearsed in the counseling session: (1) the couple prepares to fight, with irritation at the other building up until it finally breaks out in words; (2) the couple agrees to fight with both partners being willing to discuss an issue, reviewing "arms control" or ground rules of the fight. Bill says "I want to discuss our relationship to our families and not the church," and Ann agrees; (3) the fight itself. One states the problem or issue. The other gives feedback and presents his side of the issue. Each corrects the other's impressions, images, and feelings involved in the interaction. Each listens to the other side. Finally when the issue has been talked through, one or the other signals that the fight is over; (4) reconciliation. There is a mutual

---

[18] I have drawn from George Bach's fight training in this section. See *The Intimate Enemy* by Bach and Wyden, (New York: William Morrow & Co., 1969).

disengagement from the conflict. The couple make up by assessing for themselves and to each other what they have learned from the discussion. They reach out for harmony and new agreements; (5) peaceful relations are resumed. The couple live by their new agreements. They begin to practice the changes suggested under the heat of the argument. They keep the lines of communication open and are aware when a new fight is necessary. The counselor is very active in such counseling, stopping the couple when they are counterproductive and helping them to get back on the track.

Enabling. The counselor is an enabler for the couple. With Bill and Ann, the reconciling and resuming of peaceful relations have required an enabler. They could get the issues out on the table, but the negotiating of a "new role contract"—Bill allowing Ann access to his work; Ann allowing Bill to be a father of the baby in deed as well as word—has required a third party. They each trust the counselor, know he is not taking sides, and will find it possible to give as well as take in his presence. The counselor is impartial, gets nothing out of the bargaining except the indirect reward of being a part of a creative problem-solving process. When sexual relations are reinstated it is not as a reward from Ann, but rather a bridge which reunites the separate partners. Living by the new agreements needs the support of the counselor as Bill and Ann report back to him week by week. New adjustments between them are now possible as the couple have learned to quarrel constructively. The intimacy they now experience is not the lovey-dovey blindness of the honeymoon. It is a genuine caring for the other as they work through differences and find ways of sharing themselves with the other through conflict.

Marriage Growth Groups
for Ministers and Their Spouses

The marriage growth group provides a creative approach to the special problems of couples at various stages of their marriage. Marriage enrichment, marriage communication, or couples encounter group are names also associated with this kind of group. The growth group differs from the counseling or therapy group in that the purpose is not for the healing of broken persons or marriages, but the growth of healthy ones. Joseph Knowles says, "A therapeutic group provides a peer group in which each member can have (emotionally) corrective experiences." [19] Those who seek therapy in groups recognize that they do not have serious personal problems and go to a group therapist rather than an individual therapist for help.

A clergy couple who do not have problems needing marriage counseling, but simply want to grow in their marriage, may seriously consider joining a growth group. The purpose of such a group varies with the age of those who make it up, the number of years each has been married, and the nature of the marriages represented (traditional, companionate, open, closed, or whatever). However, as Howard Clinebell says so well, the growth formula is *caring + confrontation*, and with a suitably trained leader, the couple should be able to discover new ways of increasing the intimacy of their marriage.[20] As we observed earlier, the mar-

---

[19] Knowles, Joseph, *Group Counseling* (Philadelphia: Fortress Books, 1967), p. 16. Knowles uses basically a psychoanalytic approach, although I understand from personal discussion with him that he has currently adapted encounter methods in his therapy groups.

[20] Clinebell, Howard, *The People Dynamic* (New York: Harper & Row, 1972), p. 8.

riage task at each stage may need to be faced openly, and it can be confronted more easily with a caring group than it can alone. Each growth group will develop its own agenda and, with the help of its leader, develop its own group life allowing growth to take place.

Robert Leslie calls the growth group a "sharing group" and has, over several decades of experience, developed the following guidelines for the life of the group. (1) Responsibility is accepted by members for the group's life; (2) communication of feelings is sought rather than socialization among members; (3) the focus is on the present without ignoring the past; (4) personal sharing is preferred over diagnostic probing for answers; (5) attacks are discouraged, but observations are welcomed; (6) the leader is willing to share himself while remaining objective; (7) change is encouraged, but not required; (8) action beyond the group is expected and shared. The focus is on the marriage relationship in the couple's group so that the leader, or leader couple, and the group members help each couple to understand not just their feelings, but their interaction better through reflective and confrontive means. Through the use of encounter exercises, games, and sharing experiences, each couple is able to develop new ways of coping with the change and challenge of their family life.[21]

Clergy couples who are interested in joining a growth group or forming one of their own should read one of the many helpful books in the field. Robert Leslie's *Sharing Groups in the Church,* Howard Clinebell's *People Dynamic,* or Gerald and Elisabeth Jud's

---

[21] Leslie, Robert, *Sharing Groups in the Church* (Nashville: Abingdon Press, 1970), pp. 138-61.

Training in the Art of Loving, are three books specifically aimed at ways the growth group may be utilized within the church itself.[22] A word of warning about encounter groups should be sounded, however, since they have spread like a brush fire throughout the United States since the late sixties. Couples should be clear about the leader's credentials since many unqualified persons conduct groups and may do damage. The nature of the group experience should be understood since some "rage" techniques may remove defenses and open up difficulties which cannot be handled effectively in such groups. The follow-up of the experience should be assured since short-term experience among strangers may leave the couple more upset and needing of nurture and support than if they had no such experience at all. One's denominational, family-life leaders either at the state or national level should be consulted about the leadership for such groups and the possibilities explored for an interested number of couples starting such a group.[23]

Below I have condensed a session of a marriage growth group which I conducted to give some sense of the dynamics between the members and the flow of the session.

---

[22] Jud, Gerald, and Jud, Elisabeth, *Training in the Art of Loving: The Church and the Human Potential Movement* (Philadelphia: Pilgrim Press, 1972). See also Foster, Arthur L.; "The Use of Encounter Groups in the Church," and Stewart, Charles, and Hand, Quentin, "Programmed Instruction as an Aid to Marriage Counseling," *Journal of Pastoral Care*, vol. 26 (September 1972), pp. 148-65.

[23] A new national leadership group has been formed for marriage enrichment. Write Association of Couples for Marriage Enrichment, 403 South Hawthorne Rd., Winston Salem, N.C. 27103.

A Marriage Growth Group (Session 7)

We began the group with the exercise called "fish-bowl" in which wives sit in a circle with husbands standing behind them. The wives say, "The way I see men is . . ." Then the situation is reversed, and the men say, "The way I see women is . . ." The women say men are "strong, thoughtful, tender, rough, insensitive at times." The men say women are "soft, emotional, strong at times, bitchy, sexy." What happens after the exercise is that both men and women talk about sex differences and what part of the difference is due to biology and what to training. One woman, Jane, says she thinks men and women are the same, that the differences are trained into them as children. She is met with opposition, although members of the group agreed that there is a basic core of humanity not recognized because of stereotypes which they carry around with them.

The discussion moved into sexual responsiveness, and the women wanted to talk about their sexual feelings. This had been broached before, but in this open atmosphere they shared their desire for closeness with their mate and the fact that sometimes they experienced multiple orgasm (icing on the cake, one said) and at other times no orgasm, but it wasn't necessary. The men spoke of their visual-centeredness, liking a pretty body, but that sex had become for some more of a total experience and not centered in the genitals.

Sexual roles led to work role sharing. A couple in their forties felt that the wife should support the husband by church attendance and by work in the church which would reflect on him. Two couples in their twenties, however, felt that the wife should do her own thing, not go to church if she did not feel like it nor participate in the activities if it were not her desire. In particular, the group divided on whether the husband could be his wife's pastor and whether the wife could be his supervisor of counseling. All felt, however, that this was one of the difficulties that they had—there was no place for them to go to share their confidences. A couple in their first church felt the divisiveness of the congregation and that several women had taken out their anger against the wife.

Taking a stand on special issues had brought misunderstanding and difficulty for three of the six couples. The woman is not another layman in this instance in that she either stands beside her husband, or he feels doubly defeated. One wife said that this had been their solace, and the husband said he could not have stayed in the church without his wife's steady support. A thirty-five-year-old minister in a central city church recounted how he felt the congregation's support when he admitted his mistakes and his humanity and did not try to stand above them or appear to be above criticism. Even one whom he differed with most strongly agreed to disagree with him, and this kept them in the church together. On leaving, all agreed that this discussion led them to understand the spiritual underpinnings in their marriage, and that fortunately they did not have to feel they were alone—that they had the support of God in their task.[24]

---

[24] Gerard Koob, S. J. conducts Marriage Encounters for Couples over weekends utilizing written communication between couples, done in private and then shared between them before being talked about before a group. His rationale is that couples will get more honest in writing than they will when engaging in verbal communication. Reported in *Washington Post*, March 1, 1973.

Continuing Marriage Support

Clergy couples are often isolated, and in their isolation they miss the presence of another couple or couples who provide them friendship and support when crisis occurs. Some ministerial couples naturally gravitate to a friend's home on Sunday evening to relax from the week's activities and pressure. What might be suggested is that the clergy couple consciously form a group of three to six couples which would meet on a continuing basis for mutual encouragement and support. This group could be leaderless—i.e., not with professional leadership—other than the leadership represented by those in the group itself. Usually one or more ministers have engaged in clinical pastoral training or sensitivity training—at least enough to know the shoals and narrows of group life.

Fellowship is important, but lest the group become simply a coffee klatch, some conscious intent and structure will be necessary. An occasional weekend for meditation or an occasional growth group marathon at a camp or recreation setting will give the group members an additional feeling of support and connect the group more strongly. In a day when the extended family has evaporated for most urban dwellers and young people are seeking communes for support, the minister, whether married or single, should also find a network of concern and loving care to nurture him.

Continuing Education
for Ministry

Too long has a pastor been regarded as learned
because he has had extensive training. He is learned
only if he is continually learning. Some of his most
important learning comes only after ordination. His
most vital theological education will be what he
learns in the continuing present, all his mature years.

—Henry Adams, "Continuous Education
for Ministers"

Education has emerged as a major social force in
contemporary society—not just education for the young
to prepare them for a place in the working world,
but education for persons of all ages to keep them
abreast of vast social and technological changes which
affect their life work. The knowledge explosion is particularly felt by those occupations like engineering—
professors at Massachusetts Institute of Technology
say that an engineering degree will last about eight
years before it will need to be completely updated.
Physicians must continually read medical journals and
attend conferences in order to be aware of new treat-
ments and techniques. Teachers from kindergarten to
graduate school must stay abreast of their fields or
they will soon be out of a job. If this is true for these
occupations and professions, should it not also be for
the minister? In order to keep in touch with the vast
social changes happening at such a breakneck pace, he
will need to be involved in the community. In order to
understand the new changes in the theological world
and the church, one will need to go back to school from

time to time. So that one may keep in touch with one-self in relation to the profession, one will need time to get apart and reflect on what is going on introspectively. And certainly, in the light of our study thus far, as he faces professional and career development, one will need to retrain in order to meet new challenges.

Continuing education is a comparatively new development in the church, not quite two decades old. The professional organization for continuing educators, Society for Advancement of Continuing Education for Ministry, was formed in 1967; and the Roman Catholic organization, National Organization for Continuing Education of Catholic Clergy, was formed in 1973.[1] The offerings in continuing education have grown, however, like the green bay tree. With such a plethora of opportunities, it is necessary for working ministers to understand not only their own needs, but something about what continuing education is and how it may serve them professionally in order for them to become truly lifetime learners. Otherwise, they may fall victim to piece-meal offerings, which do not help them with their career—traditional lectures which merely add to their notebooks on the shelf, or a rest-and-recreation setting which gives them a temporary shot in the arm, but which will have to be repeated again soon.

Questions a Pastor Faces

The working pastor has certain questions about continuing education which are quite natural in his work setting.

1. What is continuing education, and how may it serve me?

---

[1] SACEM, 3401 Bound Brook Rd., Richmond, Va. 23227; NOCECC, 1312 Massachusetts Ave. NW., Washington, D.C. 20001.

2. What kinds of training are available? Where are the bases of training?
3. Who are the agents of training responsible for continuing education?
4. What is the relationship between the training I receive and the parish I serve?
5. What is the relationship between the training I receive and the development of my career?
6. How may I plan my training? Is there anyone available who can help me plan? Are there financial resources available?
7. How may I keep motivated for ministry? Is there a way in which getting involved in continuing education will enable me to be a productive person throughout my lifetime?

In this chapter we shall very practically look at each question in turn.

What Is Continuing Education, and How May It Serve Me?

The Roman Catholics define continuing education quite simply as "learning after ordination" and say it involves internal growth and external change. By internal growth they mean the development of a person spiritually, emotionally, and intellectually throughout his entire life. This is the continuing of priestly formation begun during seminary. The Roman Catholic priest according to the study by Eugene Kennedy has failed to grow through inertia and through the traditional concepts which he has both of priesthood and of education.[2] The need for the priest to change, particularly in the mid-years, is very dramatic say the leaders of the church. By external change they mean the changes going on in the culture, and they point out

[2] Kennedy and Heckert, *The Catholic Priesthood in the U.S.*, Psychological Investigations.

that unless the priest is aware of these changes and is adapting or adjusting to them he will not only stagnate, but also may lose his authority as a leader. By education they mean not just academic education, although this has been the emphasis of the church, but education which changes the whole man—intellectually, spiritually and emotionally.[3]

Protestants generally have defined continuing education as "that part of a leader's planned education that has its point of beginning where formal education ceases to be his primary goal in life."[4] Connolly Gamble, Executive Secretary of SACEM (The Society for the Advancement of Continuing Education for Ministry) says, "It involves not a withdrawal into the occupation of student but discovery of resources for learning while engaged in a ministerial vocation. It is education for ministry and goes on in the midst of engagement in that ministry. Whatever educational program he chooses, the program is his. It belongs to him rather than to the institutions which sponsor the various events . . . of his continuing education. . . . He chooses the study units, orders them in sequence . . . determines the depth to which they will be pursued . . . all in the light of the particulars of his situation in ministry."[5]

Continuing education for ministry is not content, skill, or therapy learning, but self-directed learning of the whole person in relation to his profession. Such education involves a stance or attitude for it to take

[3] *The Program of Continuing Education of Priests,* Washington, D.C., National Conference of Catholic Bishops, November 14, 1972.

[4] Gamble, Connolly, "A Personal Philosophy of Continuing Education," Consultation on Continuing Education for Ministers (Chicago: University of Chicago Press, 1965), p. 17.

[5] *Ibid.,* p. 18.

place. The individual should be open to new experience and have a capacity to reflect upon that experience. He should be a self-starter, which means he is not dependent now upon someone with greater authority to tell him what meets his needs. He should be able to accept constructive criticism from consultants and co-workers so that he may improve his professional practice. He should be able to work with colleague groups which will support, evaluate, and confront him with his mistakes as well as his successes. He should be able to separate his professional work from his personal and family life so that he is neither drained by his work nor smothered by his family and friends.

Continuing education will serve such a minister as he plans for it, incorporates it within his professional planning and goal setting, and utilizes its insights and supportive strengths not just for spurt-type work, but for sustained teamwork with colleagues and laymen. Continuing education is seen then not as brushing up in theology or Bible when one comes back annually for the seminary alumni lectures. It is seen as taking place at the planning level while a young man or woman is still in seminary. It is also understood as a vital part of the middle years of ministry and as one gets ready for retirement. Perhaps such planning cannot go on any longer than ten years in advance, but at least, barring accident, illness, or death, the serious professional can incorporate continuing education into his total career planning and personal development.

Where Does Continuing Education Take Place?

If you as a minister grant that you are primarily responsible for continuing to grow professionally, then you also realize that you must learn on the job. The primary place of learning after ordination is, therefore, the parish. There are specific areas in the parish and particular ways in which the minister engages in the learning process. What are these?

THE STUDY. The study has been the traditional place of learning for the working minister, where he can disengage himself from active professional life and may read, mark, and inwardly digest books, articles, and in particular the Bible. Samuel Blizzard's research in 1956 stated that the minister spent very little time in the study (thirty-eight minutes a day in sermon preparation versus sixty-four minutes a day in secretarial work).[6] Moreover, ministers complain that the time spent there is disconnected in approach, is used for topical reading to produce sermons, and touches only the surface of problems or issues. The ominous presence of the telephone and the continuous interruptions from the parish give the minister precious little time to study or to reflect on his experience and reading. The purpose of the study is to offer the active minister a chance to think, to analyze problem situations, and to attempt creative, new ways of putting one's thoughts together. I shall not go into the various means modern clergy have utilized in order to carve out a time and place for serious reading and reflection. Suffice it to say that unless today's ministers order their priorities to spend two to three hours a day in the study, they will not long remain contemporary and relevant in their work.[7]

---

[6] Blizzard, "The Minister's Dilemma," *The Christian Century* (April 25, 1956), p. 509.

[7] In preparing this manuscript I discovered it possible to find privacy in a library of medicine where no one knew me or was able to reach me for hours.

THE STAFF. Having put the traditional study first, today's minister should recognize other forms of professional learning which involve him first with other ministers and second with laymen who are members of the parish he serves. The young pastor will want to continue to learn the skills of ministry through the help of a pastoral supervisor. No doubt he began this kind of learning through field education courses while in seminary. If, after ordination, he is employed as an assistant minister on a church staff—and more young men and women start out this way—he should look to the senior pastor for such supervision. One must acknowledge, as Kenneth Mitchell says, that many senior pastors are not equipped to supervise their junior colleagues.[8] Nevertheless many senior pastors are learning the skills of supervision and are able to serve as preceptors for their young assistants. Learning involves weekly sessions of at least an hour in which the assistants enlist feedback concerning their professional work from the senior minister and then modify their role behavior with the support of the senior pastor and the others of the professional staff. It is not enough to continue to make mistakes; one should learn from one's mistakes as one moves into the profession.

THE COLLEAGUE GROUP. The colleague group is emerging in this decade as one of the most significant places for ministers to continue their learning. This group may be as small as a church staff or as large as a community ministerium. The focus of study may be a book or series of books in a particular area; more often

---

[8] Mitchell, *Psychological and Theological Relationships in the Multiple Staff Ministry* (Philadelphia: The Westminster Press, 1966).

than not the group finds its focus around professional concerns. One of the consistent discoveries of continuing educators is that practicing ministers can teach each other in the context of a colleague group.[9] Such a professional concerns group may have elements of group dynamics and may exist for the sake of each person understanding himself, his style of leadership, and his mode of interpersonal relationships. In this instance the group may be led as they are in Frankfurt, Germany by a psychiatrist.[10] In most instances the leadership comes from the group itself, and operates with the minimum of structure. Directed reading may be obtained from various continuing education centers.[11] And in many instances, resource persons will come to the group after it has completed its study for discussion of the various issues raised. If the clergyman operates within a social system, the church, what better way to continue his education than within that system itself? Moreover, if he is to engage laymen in recognizing and witnessing to their ministry, then his education should not separate him further from the laity, but be carried out with the laity.

CONSULTATION. One of the newer and more constructive methods of clergy-lay training is through parish development with the aid of a consultant. Consultation is a recognized skill, differing from supervision, in that it does not operate within a one-to-one relationship

---

[9] Rouch, Mark A., "A Risk for the Sake of Health," pamphlet published by Board of Education, United Methodist Church, Nashville, Tenn., 1972.

[10] Argelander, Herman, "Balintgruppenarbeit mit Seelsorgern". A paper read at Evangelical Academy, Arnoldshain Conference, July 20, 1972.

[11] See Richard Murray's program at Southern Methodist University, Perkins School of Theology, Dallas, Texas, as a prime example.

alone, but works within the administrative group structure of the organization. The consultant is a skilled person able to analyze and describe the functional operation of groups and to work constructively with such groups to enable them to accomplish their organizational goals. The new minister may attempt to set his administrative and organizational goals alone and not be aware of the need for the building of the organization through group process. The professional consultant may be the person who can teach him and the laity while actually going through the process of purposing, planning, working through a problem, and then evaluating. This is not an easy way of learning, as I have witnessed it, but it may be the "baptism of fire" for young ministers by which they turn from being passive, disengaged persons into active participants in the life of their parishes.[12]

SEMINARY, UNIVERSITY, AND CONTINUING EDUCATION CENTER. The second general locus for professional learning is outside the parish. This is the usual place of which the minister thinks when considering continuing education. The seminary from which he graduated will offer him continuing education opportunities of which he should take advantage. But he will also find university classes, many of them offered at night, which will often be directed at his particular area of need and interest. The continuing education center which specializes in tailored courses—from one day to six weeks in length—will bring him together with other ministers and laymen of many denominations for specialized professional work. SACEM provides an annual listing of such courses—by region—for the

---

[12] See Mead, Loren, *New Hope for Congregations* (New York: The Seabury Press, 1972).

working professional.[13] We shall return to these outside resources below when we discuss making a plan for continuing education.

Who Should Be the Responsible Agents of Continuing Education?

The mushrooming growth of continuing theological education has caused a diffusion of responsibility and a resulting confusion on the part of the average clergyman as to whom to go to for help in planning.

The primary responsibility lies with the denominational leadership of the church itself. John Harris, after considerable study and reflection upon the practices in the Episcopal Church, writes:

> We know that if the judicatory leadership fails to care and work for intelligent placement practices, pragmatic continuing education for clergy, career guidance, strong peer bonds between clergy, competent parish development consultation, then the consequence is likely to be visible in the form of depressed, unproductive pastors and apathetic churches.[14]

The denomination's leadership needs to take account of the continuing education of its leaders and, through a national agency and a network of regional boards, to implement such education. Happily, such structures are now in existence in most judicatories, with financial aid available for clergymen to use in their continuing education. At many places, however, ministers who have a career development approach need to assume

---

[13] Continuing Education Resource Guides, SACEM, 3401 Bound Brook Rd., Richmond, Virginia 23227.

[14] Harris, John C., "Pastoral Care of Pastors," *Pastoral Psychology*, vol. 22 (March 1971), p. 8.

leadership at the local level so that planning for continuing education does not remain tied to traditional concepts and methods.

Who should be the agents of continuing education at the curricular and individual course levels? The judicatory leadership should enlist the response of professional educators in the region to design courses for the clergy according to the ministers' individual, career, and parish needs. Such courses may well have ministers, Christian educators, and other religious leaders as part of the planning process. What I am suggesting is that rather than the educational curriculum fostering the usual professor-student dependency, continuing education should enlarge the minister's abilities to become a self-directed learner. He may go to the seminary professor, university professor, or human relations trainer to help him design his learning experience, but his needs and career goals should be uppermost in the planning. Theology of churchmanship, family financial planning, counseling the adolescent take a different form and shape when a dialogical and contractual approach is used by the minister-student in relation to his resource leader.

What Is the Relation
of Continuing Education to the Parish?

The parish is central in the continuing education of the minister. Having said that, we should recognize at least three patterns of relationship between continuing education and the parish.

1) The "away from the parish" programs utilize a "withdrawal and return" cycle. For many tired, disgruntled, and depressed professionals this cycle offers not only a respite from the rigors of parish duties, but

an opportunity for perspective on the parish and for reflection upon one's vocational purposes and plans. It is therapeutic (offering catharsis, insight, and renewal of purpose) for ministers to get together in a think tank and to experience Bible study, worship, mutual resource sharing, and play. However, unless some back-home planning takes place, such conferences are prefaces to more frustration when one comes down from the peak experience of the group and attempts to see the relevance for the parish of what one has experienced.

2) Reuel Howe, pioneer in continuing education for clergy, said from the beginning that clergy and laity should be trained together. In all the conferences at the Institute for Advanced Pastoral Studies, laymen are a part. A visit to laymen at their place of work in business or industry offers to ministers an opportunity both to experience the layman's world and to probe ways they have of carrying out their vocation as Christians in that world. Laymen's sermon feedback groups give ministers an opportunity to perceive what laymen hear from the pulpit and how they plan to use the gospel as preached in their daily lives. Following through such perceptions in further discussion with laity often opens a professional up to his necessary colleagueship with the laity.[15]

One of the most remarkable conferences to grow out of Howe's work has been the "Trainer of Trainers" workshop. The design of this conference was to train clergy in ways of helping the laity to recognize and to carry out their Christian vocation in the world. Enablement took on flesh and blood as clergy and lay

---

[15] The author served as an associate of Reuel Howe from 1963-1966 and made these observations first hand.

persons recognized their separate areas of expertise and through dialogue and skill training were able to see how they might better function in those areas. Connolly Gamble sees this as the central task of the church.

> Tactically the church must seek to educate leaders who will in turn become educators of others. This has been the Church's way through much of its history, and the plan is sound. It works *if* the leaders are adequately trained and *if* they carry through as teachers of others. So all study programs for churchmen ought to have this dual focus—learning in order to teach others.[16]

3) Clergy and laity can work together within the parish in planning, organizing and renewing church structures. In the process they may learn what it means to "equip God's people for work in His service" (Eph. 4:12). The use of the consultant has been mentioned as a way of renewal. Planning retreats, sharing groups, and growth groups are other means for ministers and laymen to work together. For the minister to stay alive in his work, the parish must come alive. The best continuing education of clergy, therefore, has the congregation at its heart.

What Is the Relationship Between Continuing Education and Career Development?

The question is central to the thesis of this book. Stated concisely it is: The minister's continuing education should be related to his changing career needs; i.e.,

---

[16] Gamble, "A Personal Philosophy of Continuing Education," Consultation on Continuing Education for Ministry, University of Chicago, June 1965, p. 22.

the minister should plan his education to enhance, support, and increase his personal resources so that he may be productive throughout his entire work life. Such education is posited on the premise that learning continues throughout a lifetime. Career development operates on the principle that to grow professionally one will need to enlarge his knowledge and skills or gain new areas of knowledge and skills to meet professional demands and challenges.

To make this thesis concrete, let us look at three critical periods in a minister's career and the continuing education needs of that period. We may also evaluate some programs which attempt to respond to those needs.

ESTABLISHMENT PERIOD. We examined the establishment period in chapter 4 (year one to year ten in the ministry) and the needs of the postordination years. Mark Rouch says:

> It is essentially a professional entrance crisis during the establishment phase of the career. The enthusiasm and drive evident immediately after seminary may have dissipated; learnings have been tried; the job experience has created new learning needs; the young minister may want to change jobs but sees no immediate prospect. Sometimes—not always—considerable stress develops both for the minister and his family which causes some to leave the ministry.[17]

Thomas Brown considers three basic needs of young pastors which reinforce what we discussed in chapter 4. They are: (1) the need for colleague relationships with other ministers to whom they can be responsible and

---

[17] Rouch, "A Young Pastors Pilot Project: An Experiment in Continuing Education for Ministry," *Journal of Pastoral Care*, vol. 25 (March 1971), p. 4.

from whom they draw strength, (2) the perception of the religious needs of persons in the parish—their worship needs, their needs for group expression, and their needs for community action, and (3) their recognition of the need for laymen's feedback and ways of engaging laymen in dialogue and cooperative endeavor.[18]

The Young Pastors schools, long established by Presbyterian and Lutheran bodies and more recently being formed by United Methodist and Roman Catholic groups, represent a response to these needs. To look at one, the Young Pastors Pilot Project, we discover a design built basically around three elements: (1) cluster groups of five to eight pastors which meet every two weeks for two years under the tutelage of senior pastoral associates, (2) seminars of three to four days held at the beginning, middle, and end of the project and focusing on both content and skill areas, (3) training programs for the pastoral associates so that they might better fulfill their function in the program. This program is particularly interesting to study, since an elaborate research-evaluation was done on it by Edgar Mills and his associates in published form. In summary Mills reports:

> The points at which there is convincing evidence for PP [pilot project] impact include two important areas: greater collaborative problem-solving in sensitive areas and the setting of more specific goals for ministry. There is also some evidence that the PP stimulated theological reflection, encouraged growth in competence, and focused a desire for stronger peer support and professional development structures. The remaining objectives were not met —sometimes because changes in the desired direction

---

[18] Personal communication, Lancaster, Pa., June 5, 1973.

were not observed, and in other cases because the comparison pastors appeared to change at least as much as the Young Pastors.[19]

THE MAINTENANCE PERIOD. We have also examined the career stress of mid-life among professional ministers (ages forty to fifty-five). Research with the mid-careerist in the ministry is at a minimum. However, Thomas Brown has documented the results of the study of one hundred religious professionals who sought career counseling at mid-life. He discovered the following needs: (1) a need for reestablishment and work, (2) a need for maintenance that implies an arrival which may be resisted, (3) a need to make vocational decisions, (4) a need for effective life-planning processes, (5) a need for reshuffling value orientations, i.e., from work or money to pleasure or meaning, (6) physical health problems, and (7) problems surrounding mobility and unemployment.

Conferences can be specifically designed for this group, or they may become a part of conferences in which other ages are a part. Research on a professional concerns conference, with men in their second ten years of ministry, did show some short-term educational changes, some of which were not predicted. The educational goals of the conference included changes in self-perception and interpersonal relations; however, no perceptible changes were found in these areas. The changes which occurred were in role perception, which meant that the men were able to change the stance they took within the ministry, in particular in their leadership style. They learned to accept a dialogical approach

---

[19] Mills, *Peer Groups and Professional Development*, Nashville, Tenn. Division of the Ordained Ministry, United Methodist Church (March 1973), p. 189.

with laymen and to allow laymen to exercise their ministry in the church. This stance might well have been learned at the establishment phase, but it was not because of various blocks (isolation, solo performances, and the like).[20]

PRERETIREMENT. We examined the later years also in chapter 4 and elicited the needs of the preretirement period. However, except for the early work of Paul Maves and Lennart Cedarleaf, Bernice Newgarten, and the newly emerging work of the White House Conference on Aging, not much research has been undertaken on the educational needs of this period. The novelist Dostoyevsky quoted his Underground Diarist as writing, "To live beyond 40 is bad taste," and it may well be the feeling of those who attempt to continue their education during this period. The needs are unique: (1) emotional needs surrounding the feeling that one's life is over and that all he must do is to prepare for death, (2) needs surrounding the aging process which means slowing down in one's career without quitting, (3) a need to begin to do the things one has always wanted to do, but has put off because of the press of work, (4) the need for career guidance which will help one prepare oneself for a second or third career one can carry into retirement, (5) integrity needs, which we examined earlier, but which focus on living by an energizing and life-sustaining faith and value orientation.

Continuing education programs should be designed

---

[20] Stewart, Charles W., "A Study of the Results of a Program of Continuing Education for Protestant Clergy," research report, 1966. We used a preconference postconference research design, using 17 men and matching them with a control group, keeping age, marital status, denomination, congregation size, and location constant.

specifically for this group of ministers, but not always at a theological seminary. Community college courses are often the kind which allow the preretirees to engage one another in discussion and skill training which meets their specific needs. This may well be across professional lines. Ministers will find a lot in common with professors, social workers, and even mailmen with the same interests.[21] Moreover, lest this age group feel isolated, conferences should be designed which throw them into contact with younger professionals. At the risk of the more mature individual dominating the conversation, he should have the opportunity to meet and share his professional experience with young people.

How Should the Professional
Plan His Continuing Education?

The main direction of this chapter has been toward helping the minister examine his learning needs and to plan his educational program in as intelligent a fashion as he plans his career. But how may I plan? you ask. And where do I get help and guidance in planning? Good questions! And fortunately the answers to these questions are possible to find.

Time and again, directors of continuing education centers and leaders in career guidance have told me of the need for a person whose job it would be to help ministers and religious leaders to plan their educational

---

[21] I found an Art Expression Course in which I was able to learn how to do water color painting and to do this with an art teacher, three housewives, and a business person; a Group Therapy course for Mental Health professionals in which two of us clergy participated anonymously for a semester with 6 social workers. Both were exciting learning experiences!

ventures. This person should be at the community level or at least at the regional level available to pastors who are ready to take the necessary steps to retrain, to take a study leave, or to consider what education is necessary in order to specialize in a particular phase of ministry.[22] Currently the director of a pastoral counseling center, career guidance counselor, or teacher at a continuing education center provides such counseling. But often they are not close enough to the parish to be of help. The Roman Catholic Church now frees one of its priests of extra duties in a diocese so that he may offer counsel and guidance to those wanting continuing education. Protestant churches could well do the same!

The kind of guidance offered is very practical. It may be meeting such questions as these: Should I now engage in short-range or long-range plans? Where should I obtain the skills which I feel I need at this particular phase of my career? How may I build one program on top of another so that the effect is a cumulative curriculum? Should I take a longer study leave at this time? Where may I engage in the kind of skill training I want? Should I attempt a degree program at this stage of my career, and if so, where will it lead me? Will career counseling help me get to my goals and understand what I should think of doing in the next phase of my work life? Where may I obtain financial resources to underwrite my educational program?

Mark Rouch attempted what he called "A Modest Proposal Concerning the First Decade of Ministry." The design in skeletal outline looks like this:

---

[22] A sabbatical for a minister is often 3 months in length and spaced over a three-year interval, rather than the academic 6 months every 6 years.

Phase I (First Professional degree)			Phase II (Continuing Education)		
1 - 2 - 3 -	4 -	5 -	6 - 7 -	8 - 9 -	10
Commitment to program Planning begins	Full involvement in job No school	Skill training	18-24 months young pastors-type program	Theological and/or cultural studies and/or skill training	Sabbatical

Such a design meets career crises with adequate time for reflection and study. It allows for individual differences in that some persons will feel the need for skill training and some will want additional exposure to theology or to culture. It further meets the need for study in collegial groups in the early days of one's career. It would be helpful for the reader to sit down alone or with a colleague or with an educational counselor and to think through some such plan, the better to coordinate his study and to plan his career effectively.[23]

How Does One Keep Motivated for Ministry?

Most crucial in all one's lifetime are his motives. We have examined the ambiguity the average minister encounters in the parish and his resulting confusion, loss of confidence in himself, and frustration in his attempts to do his professional work. Personal conflicts, marital problems, and career crises were the result. In this chapter we have been examining continuing education as a response to this set of problems in ministry.

We should note first that one's motives for ministry change as one gets older. Gordon Allport made us

---

[23] Rouch, "A Modest Proposal Concerning the First Decade of Education for Ministry," mimeographed paper, 1972, p. 6.

aware of how a motive to serve—perhaps egocentric and not too worthy—can become an organizing center and in adulthood become cleansed of some of the childish and adolescent origins.[24] Thus, during the early years, a person may decide to serve the church because of a desire to serve God and to reform the institution. During the middle years, many individuals find their motives becoming more humanistic and more group oriented. One does not necessarily lose theological concern although Mills and others have found expastors have become less involved in theological belief systems. For many, however, love of God and love for man become more coordinated and integrated. In serving the church, the leader becomes less a prima donna and more of a team player without losing individuality.

Today's minister will come to continuing education classes and conferences wanting to work through issues surrounding why he does what he does and how he can maintain his enthusiasm and desire to stay at his work. The program should encounter the minister at this point and help him to work through his vocational needs and aspirations with the help of good counseling and supportive group life. Moreover, each person may have his own battles with finding and releasing creativity in his work. The continuing education experience, although not therapy, should provide the support necessary for the minister to understand his strengths and talents and to prepare to employ them more usefully in his work. As the proverb states:

Give me a fish and I will eat for today;
teach me to fish and I will eat for the rest of my life.

[24] Allport, *The Individual and His Religion* (New York: The Macmillan Co., 1951), p. 64.

At times in making this survey of continuing education, I felt as if the church were Rip Van Winkle freshly awake after sleeping for twenty years during which time the American Revolution had taken place. A Roman Catholic leader made me aware of what a mammoth task pre-Vatican II trained priests have of retraining themselves for the new day in the church. So, too, Protestant leaders out of school for ten years may be phased out and increasingly out of contact with the tremendous changes sweeping through the society, the church, and social systems like the family. Industry, government, and the university are realizing the need to train leaders better to meet the new day and its challenges. Surely, the church needs to do the same for its leaders and make continuing education its number one priority.

Which Way Ministry?

The Emerging Shape of Ministry

He knows that his task is impossible. This is the paradox of paradoxes: that he as finite, fallible, and sinful man has to represent the infinite and Holy God. . . . The ultimate paradox is indeed this —that God has entrusted the treasure of His Gospel to the earthen vessel of the minister's personality. He is to reflect the restored and prefected image of God in Christ, the new Adam, the icon of the invisible God. Yet his pride, his fear, his fallibility, his rebellion are always distorting the reflection of that image.

—Huston Davies, *A Mirror of the Ministry in Modern Novels*

Let me begin with two images of the contemporary church. One is a view from a city skyscraper overlooking an area of a former ghetto. The old tenements and row houses are being razed and pushed into rubble by bulldozers and heavy scoop cranes. Along the edge of the forty-square-block area are the churches—the only buildings not to be destroyed—but now standing like sentinels in a bleak desert. The other image is of a young man sitting on the floor of a noisy auto factory before the 7:00 A.M. shift. He is speaking with the workers about negotiating for better safety conditions in the shop. He is from the Industrial Mission and because of several years' experience as a worker on the assembly line, he has the confidence of the men with whom he is talking. He does not speak of God or

Christ, but of safety and negotiations with management.

Both images reflect the paradoxical position of the church and ministry today. Religion has been sometimes conservative, sometimes radical. The institution, like the sentinel church buildings, remains fixed in the midst of change. On the other hand, the prophets have upset the social order and brought judgment upon the ingrown and unjust institutions of society, including the temple. " 'Do not suppose that I have come to abolish the Law and the prophets; I did not come to abolish, but to complete.' " (Matt. 5:17 NEB) " 'I tell you this: (about the temple) not one stone will be left upon another; all will be thrown down.' " (Matt. 24: 1–2 NEB) Both are sayings of Jesus in his ministry.

The problems which have emerged in this investigation are rooted in the fact that ministers are not simply professionals, but are leaders of institutions with real estate, investments, and concern for maintaining perpetuity. The ministry will not reform, in fact, cannot reform until the church reforms. The conflict with the social system—the local church, the bureaucracy—will eventuate in standoffs until something is done about the entire organism. The social system must be renewed for the ministry to be renewed. If the clergy operates on the basis of absolute norms which do not touch ground with the institutional realities of the church as she exists, there develops a widening gap between clergy and laity. If the laity, on the other hand, continue to foster old stereotypes of what a minister is and does and what the church exists to do, there will be increasing unhappiness on the part of both clergy and laity.

The purpose of the church is to become a caring

community announcing and embodying the rule of God in society. Its leaders, both clergy and lay, should combine toughness and tenderness in their persons and fidelity and flexibility in their roles. Love and justice are not simply ideals, but have been enfleshed in the person of Jesus Christ and announced as the dynamic of his new society. The church through its two millenia of history has found ways of organizing its bodies so that they in some way carry on the ministry of Jesus Christ. It should be in the plan of God for this to continue in this highly complex, yet highly resourceful era.

However, if the church's leaders become frightened for their lives or cowed into silence for fear of losing their jobs, the church will not renew itself. If the community becomes so secularized in its message and its methods that the gospel is no longer announced or heard or embodied, the church as a distinctive institution will vanish. There should be tension between professional leader and laymen, but it should be a creative tension. The minister functions within the institution, flexible to changes and yet faithful to his call and to those functions of ministry which he considers part of his vocational identity. The layman functions within the society, fulfilling there his vocation as a Christian, and supporting the church as the small society where he finds an identity with fellow Christians. Supporting the minister means not simply providing an economic livelihood, nor supporting the mission of the church, but finding with him the meaning of discipleship in the present age. Nurturing laymen means not standing apart from them, but joining them in working through significant issues, as the industrial missioner was doing on the floor of General Motors.

What are some of the directions of ministry in the last quarter of the twentieth century? Another way of asking the question of yourself is: To what forces should I bend, and to what forms should I remain faithful? Still another way: What are the ways my ministry and the church-in-mission stay alive to the redemptive and renewing spirit of God? I shall put these statements as certain hypotheses, some of which are backed by observation and research and some of which are projections of trends which appear to me to be obvious today.

HYPOTHESIS 1. The ministry is not dying. There will continue to be a need for professional church leaders for as long as society allows for the existence of voluntary groups.

What this hypothesis is saying is that so long as there is freedom for Christian groups (churches) to form, there will be Christian leaders. In an urban technological society where education becomes the avenue to increasing competence and responsibility, the leaders of the church should be professional, i.e., theologically educated with identifiable skills and responsible not simply to their peers, but to their clients and bound by a service ethic.[1]

Two researcher-educators reach this conclusion from studying different groups. James Ashbrook, after studying the split between Protestant clergy and laity with regard to social reform says, "Today it seems that both rejectors and adaptors are becoming more sophisticated in recognizing the kind of institutional necessity. . . . The issue is no longer institution or no institution but what kind of institution? No longer no form

---

[1] Wagoner, Walter, "Seminary: Staging Area for Career," *Ministry Studies*, vol. 3 (May 1969), p. 23.

or new form but what forms, no longer structure or no structure, but what structures?" [2]

D'Arcy and Kennedy point out that the new priest must come to terms with the authoritarian structure of the church. They say, "To gain authority, the priest must become an increaser not a strainer, controller, to allow strong men and women to grow to the full measure of their manhood in Jesus Christ." [3] This profession recognizes the institution as a force not a form. The professional works within it as a growing, breathing organism, a social group whose life is not dependent on the minister, but which looks to him for guidance and service as he opens up their vocation as Christians and their mission in the world.

The structure of professional ministry has been threefold: (1) parish ministry, (2) para-parish or specialized ministry, and (3) nonstipendiary ministry. The direction of congregations has been toward consolidation, regrouping into more viable denominational and community units, and in some instances closing down where no longer needed or functional. Without going into the pros and cons of such activities, let us simply predict that the viable parishes will slim down, become more functional and more grass-rooted.[4] Some working pastors like Gordon Cosby see a parish of one hundred committed members as the best working unit; others organize a large parish of one thousand members into functional units for study, worship, and

---

[2] Ashbrook, "Ministry Studies," vol. 2 (October 1968), p. 33.

[3] D'Arcy and Kennedy, *The Genius of the Apostolate* (New York: Sheed and Ward, 1965), p. 228.

[4] By "grass-rooted" I do not mean suburban green, or country green, or even inner-city green concrete, but a church which lives closer to people's life issues.

service which allow for both a large worship unit and smaller study units. The parish has tended in North America toward centered communities rather than geographical units, as in Europe and South America.

Parish ministers will in the future operate as teams having functional specialties in both large and small congregations. Staff and team ministries will continue to form across denominational lines in both city and rural areas with this cooperation reflecting practical necessity as well as theological collegiality. The need for support groups among peers (see chapter 6) will continue to be a reason for cooperation between clergy of all faiths. Where teams are not possible, cluster ministries with the pooling of resources—both financial and personal—will make for greater effectiveness.

The para-parish or specialized minister will take his place alongside other professionals and will be looked upon as a faith and value consultant.[5] The chaplain of a university or hospital will need to find an identity clearly within the church in order to speak precisely for the faith within the institution and not to be absorbed into its structure as teacher or therapist. Signs on the horizon indicate that these institutions are questioning the roles of chaplains, and that the roles will need clarification or the professional will run the risk of being phased out. The denominational administrator has had his ordination questioned by some since he clearly does not have a parish or a specialized ministry. However, even this bureaucratic atmosphere may call for a minister-specialist who is theologically trained and able to bring his training to bear on policy formation and execution at the highest

---

[5] Ziegler, Jesse, editorial, *Theological Education*, vol. 9 (Fall 1972), p. 28.

levels of the church. The missionary—the outsider working in a different culture—will continue, but in a more clearly prescribed and limited way, offering consultation and specialized ministries among new and nationally indigenous churches.[6]

Finally, the worker-priest or tent-making minister will offer a place for those prophetic persons for whom the institution has not or perhaps cannot change quickly enough to offer them a viable career. An Episcopal study of twelve hundred of its clergy came to the following conclusions: "The non-stipendary style of ministry could be used by the church to develop new ministries for reaching people outside the parish—in cells, in office buildings, ministries to professionals, at educational institutions, in ghettos, urban areas, etc. . . . Whatever structure emerged, the non-stipendiary form of ministry would give the church a flexibility which it presently lacks." [7]

In all this one should not deny the ministry of the laity its proper place. When some men and women demit the ministry, i.e., renounce their ordination vows, they are no less Christian. When they join the congregation as laymen and take secular jobs or when some priests or nuns take spouses, that can be for them a Christian calling. Perhaps it will be more possible for them to do what they perceive as God's will without the weight of the institution about them. However, they must now work in a business or a school or even

---

[6] See *Persons in Mission* (mimeographed), published by Research and Development Committee of World Division, Bd. of Global Ministries, United Methodist Church, New York, N.Y. 10027

[7] Quoted in Schwartz, John C., "Modern Tentmaking: A New Leadership," *Christian Century*, vol. 90 (February 7, 1973), p. 173.

live in a commune where they will need to come to terms with others' expectations of them and to respond within social roles in order to work and relate at all.

HYPOTHESIS 2. The traditional roles of ministry will be redefined for greater flexibility to meet the demands of a changing society.

Samuel Blizzard identified preaching and pastoral care as two traditional roles of the professional minister. There is no doubt that in the twenty-five years since I began the practice of ministry, both roles have changed dramatically. The princes of the Protestant pulpit—Fosdick, Buttrick, Sockman, and Sherer, not to mention Sheen and Coughlin of the Roman Catholic Church—have passed from the scene, and where are their replacements? The great drawing power of Billy Graham and Oral Roberts is to the conservative and charismatic groups and not to the liberal, even middle-of-the-road layman.[8] When the preacher was the best educated, most highly informed, and most inspired person in the congregation, people would flock to hear him. But in a population suffering an overload of stimuli from the mass media, who needs even another hour of words?

Research has shown the non-communicativeness of much preaching and the lack of response on the part of passive audiences. Ronald Parsons in a study of twelve Detroit audiences found that only eight percent see the sermon as an event in which their participation or contribution is needed. Meeting with congregations immediately following the service, less than one-

---

[8] See Larry L. King's review of *The Preachers* by James Morris, St. Martins Press, 1973, *New York Times Book Review* (August 5, 1973), p. 4.

third were able to express a reasonably clear statement of the central thesis of the sermon.[9]

This bore out the research of others who discovered that the form of preaching got in the way of content of preaching.[10] Moreover, the primacy of the pulpit may block a congregation's studying the Scripture and thinking through their faith. The minister may not be any the less prepared to allow, even to encourage, the congregation to study the text and correlate it with issues from their experience. First Congregational Church, Berkeley, California and East Harlem Protestant Parish's practice of pre-sermon study groups offer examples of the way laymen may make input into the sermon *before* it is preached. George W. Weber says, such a sermon has a doxological element, being offered by a congregation in the praise of their life together to God for his illumination for the days ahead. I shall not elaborate on dialogical sermons, worship-in-the-round, role play, and sermon feedback groups as others have spelled out these innovations. What the average preacher needs to do is not stand "a foot above criticism"—in the pulpit—but to open his preaching to both the cleansing of the Word of God and the response of laymen involved with life issues. In such a way will the traditional means of communicating in the church move from a place of isolation to a more responsive place in the life of the congregation.

The pastoral role is the second traditional role which has undergone profound changes. In my ministry, I had to go to graduate school, immediately following

---

[9] Parsons, Ronald, "Lay Perception and Participation in the Communication of the Sermon," Ph.D. dissertation, Boston University, 1966.

[10] Thompson, William, *A Listener's Guide to Preaching* (Nashville: Abingdon Press, 1966).

seminary, to learn the new counseling role of the pastor. I have seen pastoral care shift in that quarter century from just simply calling from house to house and routine hospital visiting to a sophisticated set of skills taught to seminarians and learned in supervised clinical training. The majority of these skills have been learned from the mental health professions—psychiatry, psychology, and social work—with the temptation being to identify with these professions.

What now is emerging among Protestant and Roman Catholic pastors alike is a sense of their professional identity as pastors. Congregations help by not delegating all pastoral care to one or two ministers, but by understanding that the congregation is an agent of pastoral care. People get sick in community; they get well in community. They fall into sin in community; they are saved in community. If a pastor tries to plumb the well of human need in a congregation, he may, like John Braun, be flooded by it and run to the limit of his resources if not his sanity. However, since New Testament times, the congregation has shared grief, borne each others burdens, and found means of mutually caring for one another. The pastor as shepherd, i.e., overseer of a caring community, is not too much for one or two or more of a professional staff to bear. And the role offers a unique function not borne by other professionals. The mental health professionals in the congregation may consult with the pastors about the various problems encountered in the congregation and offer this as their lay ministry. The pastor, on the other hand, may work alongside the other mental health professionals in a clinic where he is a specialist in the theological-moral problems and serves as representative of the Christian community.

The pastor's emerging role, then, comes from his

listening-sensitivity skills within a unique theological specialist role. Hilda Goodwin, social worker, underlines this from her many years of supervision of clergymen at Marriage Council of Philadelphia: "The encounter between the clergyman and the parishioner occurs within a structure different from that of the psychological profession with its own value, goals and limitations . . . essentially the clergy are involved in helping persons develop values that will give meaning and purpose to life within the specific religious community of which they are members." [11] Whether this means that the pastor can engage in private practice is a much debated question. My position is that the pastoral counselor is one who works within the context and sponsorship of a church. He may see nonchurch persons for which fees are charged, but the service is basically offered by the parish to the community and not by the specialist to a group of clients. The research of Lowell Colston still speaks strongly to me and echoes my practice; i.e., the problems identified in pastoral counseling and the results obtained are different even though some of the methods may be similar to those practiced by other psychotherapists. [12] The support of a caring community provides the context for pastoral counseling, and when the pastor leaves that context, he is in my book no longer pastoral. How that role grows, therefore, depends as much on the dialogue between theology and the behavioral sciences as it does on the adoption of the latest therapeutic techniques.

---

[11] Goodwin, Hilda, "Dilemmas Confronting the Supervisor in Theological Education," *Theological Education*, Summer Supplement, 1969, p. 503.

[12] Colston, Lowell, and Hiltner, Seward, *The Context of Pastoral Counseling* (Nashville: Abingdon Press, 1961).

HYPOTHESIS 3. The contemporary roles of ministry will be informed and chastened by the Christian faith so as to fulfill the purposes of the church.

Samuel Blizzard rightly concluded that the roles of administrator and organizer come from secular sources and do not have biblical equivalents. They do, however, have origins within the Christian community as overseer or bishop, and the roles have been defined from the early church councils to the latest denominational disciplines. Since Blizzard's research, the bringing of sensitivity training, group dynamics, and community organization into ministerial training has enabled ministers to have a new understanding of the role of administrator and organizer.

The role of overseer or leader is a necessary one for a group. James Anderson points out the influence of the designated leader. "It has been shown that the designated leader of a group is the primary keeper of the organization's norms. That is he has most power to change the prescribed and accepted ways of behaving in the system. At the same time, the leader is the person most influenced by—most conforming to—the norms of the organization. The leader is both keeper of, and kept by the culture of his organization." [13] The authority of the minister has traditionally come from the office (through ordination, being called by a congregation, and being placed in charge of a church). Leadership studies show that laymen give this person authority as they recognize his competence and skills in working with them in the various task and teaching groups. Leadership skills are not simply innate, something one is born with. They are learned and are being

---

[13] Anderson, James, *To Come Alive* (New York: Harper & Row, 1973), p. 39.

taught at theological schools and in various group laboratories. The purpose of such leadership is to help a group clarify and undertake commonly accepted goals which further the purpose of the Christian church. Learning skills in a group life lab which enable one to manipulate a congregation to do one's bidding will not effect genuine change or benefit the church. An enabler and equipper is more than a democratic leader, as useful as that may be. It is within the context of the Christian faith that Paul says the minister is "to equip God's people for work in his service, to the building up of the body of Christ" (Eph. 4:12 NEB).

Is the new emphasis on ministerial group work simply leadership training? Yes and no! When one is involved in a parish conference, one recognizes one is using leadership skills and ways of helping an organization work toward its goals in much the same way one might work in a business organization. However, the goals of the Christian church are different, and the ethos of the group is different. Anderson rightly says, "The Church has claimed . . . that our organization is fundamentally related to the ultimate dimension of life—to the revealed truth of what man is meant to be." [14] The goals of the church reflect such transcendent claims, and its members are related as though members of a family. The dual job of equipper is to help the group keep its goals attuned to the transcendent, and yet aware of the necessity of moving in directions which are possible within its social context.

The teaching role has also become more enlightened in recent years, particularly with the advent of small

---

[14] Anderson, *To Come Alive*, p. 27. See also Anderson, Philip, *Making Church Meetings Matter* (Boston: Pilgrim Press, 1970).

groups in the church. As Robert Raines says, "The Small Group is a medium through which God has evidently chosen to help people start growing and continue to grow in Christ." [15] A minister without a knowledge of group dynamics today is like a doctor without a knowledge of antibiotics. Sensitivity training, encounter methods, and awareness exercises may change, but the trend toward making learning growth oriented will not.

Does this mean the church is in the personal growth business? Yes and no! The trained minister and/or layman may provide the setting, structure, and leadership for personal growth groups. However, the informing purpose of the church and its sustaining ethos make these groups different. Some methods will not be used, in particular those which destroy personality and those values (love, fidelity, good will) central to the Christian community. The struggle between self-realization and self-sacrifice is central to the group life within the church. Helping rejecting and rejected persons move to an awareness of God's loving acceptance and to an acceptance of others within a growth group may illuminate the gospel for persons and open them to mission.

Education is chastened and enlightened through the enlivening power of group discussion. Reflecting upon the gospel in the light of one's experience leads persons to make two responses: (1) worship, i.e., facing the center of life and meaning, and (2) service, i.e., facing up to one's responsibilities to the larger community. The minister's role as teacher is to equip and sensitize groups to face in both directions—at one time to be

---

[15] Raines, *New Life in the Church* (New York: Harper & Row, 1961), p. 79.

aware of the worship dimensions of their experience, and another to see the larger implications of their insight for mission. Rather than rote teaching, such a minister sees the equipping role as involving life issues, and enabling persons to grow to their full potential as children of God and to their inheritance as disciples to the larger community. Laymen will join him in this professional task; however, the task and teaching role of the minister will be central in the days ahead.

HYPOTHESIS 4. The experimental ministries will not exist apart from congregations; experiment will become an important part of those congregations which find their mission in the community.

The *change-agent* role of ministry is not new, although it has come to ascendancy recently in the experimental ministries. Martin Marty says:

> The norm of any description of Christian ministry is the ministry of Jesus Christ . . . it is always a ministry which is an agency of change . . . our reading of the Gospels reveals that Jesus never left a situation as he found it. Even where he was ineffective, even where he failed, even when he did not get through to someone he did not leave things as they were. He left unrest, bad conscience, uncertainty. He never failed to seek to make all things new. Where judgment was necessary he was an agent of change as the critic of the existing norms including some of the conservative institutions like the religious ones. He never failed to look at his immediate environment without seeing in it some need for redemption.[16]

---

[16] Marty, Martin in DeWire, Harry, *The Guidance of Ministerial Candidates*, Washington, D.C. Ministry Studies Board, 1966.

Jesus' parable of the vine and the branches (John 15:1-7) helps us understand the necessity for renewing forces to be anchored within a parent organization. My studies of experimental ministries in Washington, D.C., since 1966 may help put this hypothesis both critically and constructively. First, critical observations:

—An experimental minister or staff cannot be funded by a national organization independent of local sponsorship without disaster ensuing. Marketplace Ministries was a well worked out and researched concept in which a "storefront ministry" would be expanded to include offices for counseling, day nursery, and theater group. Large lists of volunteers were organized; the day nursery and theater functioned well. However, the response from laymen within neighboring churches never materialized. The result was failure, with a large debt for the national church of over a million dollars.[17]

—An experimental ministry may discover a mission group to which to minister, but in its zeal fail to bring a congregation along to share such a ministry. My evaluation research of a street ministry, funded by The United Presbyterian Church in the U.S.A., and located in the Dupont Circle area of Washington, D.C., revealed an outstanding personal ministry by Tom Murphy to "street people" which eventuated in a Runaway House, a coffeehouse, a crisis telephone center, and drug treatment center. However, the research also revealed that the ministry revolved too much around Murphy and did not involve laymen in the parent church enough for it to become the congrega-

---

[17] Market Place Ministries, reported in *Church in Mission* (January 1969), p. 7.

tion's ministry. Incidentally, Murphy discovered that the ministry to runaway adolescents took him to the suburbs where conditions in schools and affluent, but absentee parents had to be faced for the runaway and drug problem to be reached. This may argue for community coordination of such a ministry.[18]

—An experimental church may develop two congregations—one traditional and one experimental with the minister put into the impossible position of ministering to opposing groups—black versus white, middle class versus poor, those who see the purpose of the church as worship versus those who see its purpose as social action. If anything has killed such ministries it has been the development of this kind of institutional and professional schizophrenia.

Now, the constructive observations:

—Renewing forces move whole congregations to become change agents when they see their mission to the world and undertake it. The Church of the Savior may appear to have too elitist an approach to membership for the average congregation. However, Gordon Cosby's vision of every member being on mission is not elitist, but a necessity for genuine church renewal. The minister himself cannot engage in social action alone. This is the conclusion of Jeffrey Hadden and others who have traced the split between clergymen on civil rights and other liberation movements in recent years. However, it is Cosby's experience that when individual laymen and committed groups take as mission doing something about slum housing or innercity education or an international university, something happens. And

---

[18] Stewart, C. W., "Research-evaluation of the Street Ministry of Thomas Murphy" (mimeographed), Washington, D.C., 1970.

it vitalizes not just the church, but the community in which the church is set.[19]

—Liturgical renewal is linked to the vitality and increased commitment of a Christian group. William Wendt's ministry at St. Stephen's and the Incarnation is a story of a parish come alive to the needs of the innercity. Yet Father Wendt says the most important aspect of his parish is its life of celebration and its celebration of life.[20] The important matter in contemporary worship is not simply guitars and banners which reflect joy, but the radical means by which the group moves from the peripheral to the central, to confronting God and being confronted by him. Out of such responsiveness and awareness within a caring community comes renewal.

—The experimental congregation is not afraid to ritualize meaningful events within its life, some of which have a history within the Christian church, some of which do not. Ritual, rather than compulsive behavior, is a means for individuals and the group to get in touch with its depths and to respond to its center and energizing spirit. So baptism and Holy Communion are important to its life, but so are the means the congregation finds to celebrate significant "life-passages" which it lives through.

The Shape of Ministry

The ministry will change as the church changes to meet the challenges from the society. The parameters

---

[19] O'Connor, Elizabeth, *Call to Commitment,* (New York: Harper & Row, 1968).

[20] "Crunch in the Churches," by Hamblin, D. J. An account of Fr. Wendt and the Church of St. Stephen's and the Incarnation is included, *Life Magazine,* 65:79-82. Oct. 9, 1968.

of such changes are within the purpose of the Christian church and the tradition of the Christian faith. We have dealt with the traditional, the contemporary, and the experimental roles of the ministry. Let us put them together to see the emerging shape.

In the decades ahead, the ministry will be less associated with the vice-president of a business and more closely associated with the foreman of a group of workers or the teacher of a night school class. Servanthood (ministry) will be understood not as taking care of an institution, but as overseeing a caring community which is in mission. The parish will be defined as the core of committed disciples who find a network of interest and concern within a highly mobile functional group.

Within such a community, the minister will serve as *communicator*. This implies preaching and teaching, i.e., interpreting life in the world in the light of the gospel. He will be dialogical, i.e., in continual conversation with the committed, the seekers, and the nurturant group about the real issues of their lives. The vast number of stimuli reaching people from the mass media will sensitize minister and people to the need for selecting out noise and finding deeper levels of communication. The message of salvation will be communicated through spoken, written, acted, danced, and other expressive forms, but always in ways to enhance not limit personal freedom and growth in community.

Second, the minister will become a *counselor* to persons with genuine needs. This implies pastoral care to persons in relationship. The minister will not be a junior psychiatrist, but will become an expert in dealing with existential questions. He will nurture meaning in people's lives and enable them to grow to their full selfhood as sons and daughters of God. He will enable the congregation to become an agent of pastoral care to one another and a healing agent within the community.

Third, the minister will be a *change agent,* both within the church and within the area in which he works. The prophetic role is one which is more than social functionary, but is a sensitizing role within the congregation. He will sensitize laymen to the ethical issues within community life and help groups to think their way through to remedial action. Change agentry is also shared with other members of the community; however, the minister is primarily a reconciler, in the vanguard of the movement for human rights.

Fourth, the minister will be a *consultant* to the laity within the church organization and also in the layman's mission to the world. Consultation involves administration, i.e., creative problem solving within church groups. It also involves equipping laymen for service both within the body ecclesia and the body politic. Such consultation recognizes that the minister's primary sphere is the church, whereas the primary sphere of laymen is the world.

Finally, the minister will be a *celebrator* of the significant events in the life of the congregation. The priestly role is enhanced by the setting apart of one to lead in the celebration of baptism and the Lord's Supper. However, each Christian is a priest and should be called out to life in community which seeks to enact the most significant events before God and one another. The celebration of life within a caring community calls for a celebrant, who in his ordained role brings the tradition into the midst of a seeking group. Creed, symbol, and ritual are shared with the congregation as members seek and find a life of commitment and find new ways of expressing the depths and meanings of their lives.[21]

This is not a counsel of perfection, but a statement of faith and vision that the ministry offers men and women a career which will call out the best in them as well as challenge them to personal renewal throughout their lifetime.[22] The church needs leaders today. Neither institutional caretakers nor iconoclastic rebels will find the career satisfying. Creative, flexible, yet faithful persons who can work in concert with laymen to generate creative communities may have problems, but will find working in the church gratifying. Houston Davies says the task is impossible. In the light of our study, the minister who tries to hold the church on his back like an Atlas will break down or drop out. But the minister who recognizes his humanity and his need for a caring community and for a renewed and renewing faith will not just survive. He will find the support which he needs both human and divine and will be able to lead the flock to fulfill the ministry to which God has called them.

---

[21] See the list of skills necessary to fulfill these functions as worked out by a special committee and revised by the Board of the Academy of Parish Clergy, June 1972. *The Journal of the Academy of Parish Clergy*, vol. 3 (May 1973), p. 75.

[22] See also, Biersdorf, Jack, "New Wine in Old Wineskins and Vice Versa," *The Journal of Applied Behavioral Science*, vol. 9, (1973), pp. 305-20.

Index

Celibacy, 95–96
Children of the minister, 108–9
Christian "calling," 32
Christiansen, Carl, 43
Church of the Savior, Washington, D.C., 162
Church, purpose of the, 147–48
Clinebell, Charlotte, 49, 104
Clinebell, Howard, 49, 104, 118, 119
Conflicts
    See also Career conflicts; Career development conflicts
    of clergy couples, 106–12
    of the professional, 79–88
Continuing education, 124–45
    definition of, 126–28
    in early ministry, 137–39
    in late career, 140–41
    in mid-career, 139–40
    outside the parish, 132–33, 134
    parish relationship to, 134–36
    plan for, 143 (diagram)
    planning for, 128, 136–37, 141–43
    relationship to career development of, 136–41
    responsibility for, 133–34
    types of, 128–33
Continuing Education Center at Virginia Seminary, 91
Continuing education centers, 55–56
Colleague group, 130–31
Colston, Lowell, 156

Congregation in mission, 162–63
Consultant to a parish, 131–32
Contemporary church, 146–47
Coping, 47, 74
Cosby, Gordon, 150, 162
Counseling center
    See Pastoral counseling center; Career counseling center; Career development center
Craft, definition of, 23

D'Arcy, Paul F., 150
Davies, Huston, 146
Denominational official, 81–82
Developmental crises, 46–51
Developmental problems of ministers, 51–66
Developmental tasks, 48–51, 78
Directions of ministry, current, 149–63
Dittes, James, 38, 52, 56
Divorced minister, 111–12
Douglas, William, 100–102
Dropout of ministers, 43–44
Duvall, Evelyn, 103

Early ministry, 26–27, 75–76
    See also Continuing education in early ministry
East Harlem Protestant Parish, 154
Education of ministers
    See Theological education

Vatican II, 145

Washington Pastoral Counseling Center, 112
Wendt, William, 163
Wesley, John, 68
Wheelis, Allen, 48, 71
White, William, 107
Wife of the minister, 100–103
See also Family of the minister
Williams, Daniel Day, 21
Women in the ministry, 40–41

Work, definition of, 23
Work life. *See* Career
Working wife, 101–3

Young pastors. *See* Early ministry
Young Pastors Pilot Project, 138
Young pastors schools, 138
Young, Richard, 43

Ziegler, Jesse, 151